T0248268

The Battles of Fort Watson and Fort Motte, 1781

Small Battles

Mark Edward Lender and James Kirby Martin, Series Editors

The Battle of Gloucester, 1777
by Garry Wheeler Stone and Paul W. Schopp

The Battle of Harlem Heights, 1776
by David Price

The Battle of Musgrove's Mill, 1780
by John Buchanan

The Battle of Upper Sandusky, 1782
by Eric Sterner

The Battles of Connecticut Farms and Springfield, 1780
by Edward G. Lengel

The Battles of Fort Watson and Fort Motte 1781

STEVEN D. SMITH

Westholme Publishing, LLC
904 Edgewood Road
Yardley, Pennsylvania 19067
Visit our Web site at www.westholmepublishing.com

ISBN: 978-1-59416-424-8
Also available as an eBook.

Printed in the United States of America.

To Doraine and Luther Wannamaker

Contents

Illustrations

A gallery of halftones follows page 36:

Series Editors' Introduction

WE ALL HAVE HEARD and likely read about the big battles of the American Revolution. Names like Trenton, Saratoga, and Yorktown resonate in our ears. But what about all the smaller battles that took place by the hundreds, often fought away from but related to the bigger battles? It is the contention of this series that these smaller actions, too often ignored, had as much impact, if not more, in shaping the outcome of the American War of Independence.

These engagements were most often fought at the grassroots level. They did not directly involve His Majesty's professional forces under the likes of Generals William Howe, John Burgoyne, and Henry Clinton, or Continentals under Generals George Washington, Nathanael Greene, or Horatio Gates for that matter. Such smaller battles involved local forces, such as patriot militia and partisan bands of Loyalists, or at times Native Americans, mostly, but not always, fighting on the British side.

Quite often the big names were not there in such smaller-scale combat. Private Joseph Plumb Martin, writing in his classic memoir, recalled his fighting at Forts Mifflin and Mercer during November 1777. He and his comrades were trying to block British war and supply vessels moving up the Delaware River from reaching the king's troops under Sir William Howe, who had captured Philadelphia. Had they prevailed and cut off this obvious supply route, Howe might well have had to abandon the city. But no, they did not succeed. Superior British firepower finally defeated these courageous American fighters.

What bothered Martin, besides so many good soldiers being seriously wounded or killed, was not the failed but valiant effort to cut off Howe's primary supply line. Rather, writing thirty years later, what particularly irked him was that "there has been but little notice taken of" this critical action. Martin was sure he knew why: "The reason of which is, there was no Washington, Putnam, or Wayne there. . . . Such [circumstances] and such troops generally get but little notice taken of them, do what they will. Great men get great praise, little men, nothing."

While Martin's blunt lament is unusual in the literature of the Revolution, the circumstances he described and complained of are actually fairly obvious. Although often brutal, the smaller engagements too frequently have received short shrift in popular narratives about the conflict. Nor have the consequences of these various actions been carefully studied in relation to the bigger battles and the outcomes of the War for Independence more generally. Small battles accounted for the lion's share of the combat that occurred during the American Revolution. The purpose of this series is to shine a bright new light on these smaller engagements while also getting to know those lesser persons who participated in them, and grappling with the broader consequences and greater meaning of these actions on local, regional, and nation-making levels.

In the end, a more complete understanding of the Revolutionary War's big picture will emerge from the small-battles volumes that make up this series. If, as recent scholarship tells us, local history "allows us to peer deep into past societies and to see their very DNA," the Small Battles Series will do the same for the American War of Independence.

The fighting in the South during the spring of 1781 was as brutal and confusing as any during the War for Independence.

Steven Smith's book looks at four critical weeks in April and May which saw patriot forces besiege and capture Forts Watson and Motte in South Carolina. The forts were British outposts between the larger British position at Camden and the principal royal garrison in Charleston, and the loss of the forts marked a turning point—perhaps the turning point—in what became the faltering British southern campaign. In early May the patriot war effort appeared stalled. Major General Nathanael Greene, commander of southern Continental forces, frustrated after the setback at the Battle of Hobkirk's Hill, contemplated resigning his commission. But on May 10, 1781, Fort Motte fell to patriot forces under South Carolina militia brigadier Francis Marion, the famous "Swamp Fox," and Continentals under Colonel Henry—"Light Horse Harry"—Lee. The British never regained the initiative, quickly abandoning Camden and beginning an inexorable retreat to Charleston. Smith relates the details of the sieges and, significantly, places them not only in the larger context of Greene's campaign in South Carolina, but also in the milieu of the crucial civilian support network behind the patriot troops. There is an emphasis on the performance of Marion and Lee, whose ability to meld the strengths of Marion's militia and Lee's regulars was testimony to the maturing patriot war effort. Today we would call it "compound" or "combined warfare"—the effective linking of regular and irregular forces—and Fort Motte was one of the best examples of how patriots made the most of the military resources available to them. Writ small, Fort Motte reflected the wider track toward patriot success in the South.

Mark Edward Lender
James Kirby Martin
Series editors

Prologue

IT WAS THURSDAY, APRIL 12, 1781, and once again, partisan warrior Brigadier General Francis Marion, the "Swamp Fox," was dangerously close to being trapped by the British.[1] Camped at Alston's Plantation on Wahee Neck, South Carolina, Marion learned that a large, combined force of British regulars and Loyalists under the command of Lieutenant Colonel John W. T. Watson were on Catfish Creek, about five miles away (Figure 1). Behind Marion to the west was the Great Pee Dee River, which he had recklessly crossed at Burch's Ferry a few days prior. Nevertheless, he had crossed, accompanied by his exhausted partisans. Although he had maybe as many as five hundred men, the ranks were daily diminishing, and they only carried two or three rounds of ammunition per man. They were low on gunpowder and food, and out of salt.[2] To compound matters, before crossing, Marion had rashly proclaimed that anyone who he drafted into his force, but refused to join, would have their names published as "Enem[ies] to the State," their property seized, and given to "friends of America."[3]

Unfortunately for Marion, there were few friends of America at that time. Most of those not with Marion had dispersed and were in hiding as a result of two recent British raids through the heart of what had been Marion's community of support surrounding Snow's Island, South Carolina. One raid from British-held Camden, led by Lieutenant Colonel Welbore Ellis Doyle, found and destroyed Marion's depot on Snow's Island. The other, under Watson, marched north out of Georgetown, straight up through Britton's Neck, past Snow's Island, and were now along Catfish Creek. Upon learning of Marion's proclamation, Watson had wisely seized the political high ground by declaring to the Pee Dee inhabitants his peaceful intentions. In his proclamation he declared that "whereas Marion insisted upon their turning out in arms-we [British] only desired them to stay at home, & cultivate their Lands, & that every man found at home might rely upon protection."[4] This was essentially what the rebels wanted when the British invaded the backcountry after the fall of Charleston in May 1780. Had they been allowed to stay home, the British might have had South Carolina under their thumb. Instead, the British insisted that the rebels not only cease their rebellion, but that they also join the British in rounding up and subduing those rebels still in the field. That demand only strengthened the rebel resolve, especially those inhabiting the Williamsburg and Pee Dee districts including the Snow's Island region of the Great Pee Dee River. Marion had taken command of those disaffected rebels back in August 1780 and through the fall and winter of 1780–1781 harassed the British in a series of skirmishes and raids across eastern South Carolina.

Indeed, Marion had become quite a pest to the British by April 1781. Throughout the fall and winter of 1780–1781, however, British attention on Marion had been diffused by a multitude of partisan groups led by the likes of Thomas Sumter, Elijah Clarke, Isaac Shelby, and John Sevier, to name a few. Marion had survived, even sometimes thrived in the northeastern part of the state, ambushing the British at Great and Blue Savannahs, surprising them at Black Mingo and Tearcoat Swamp, and hiding around Snow's Island when necessary. Yet, eventually, greater events and maneuvers had finally set the stage in March 1781 for the British to focus

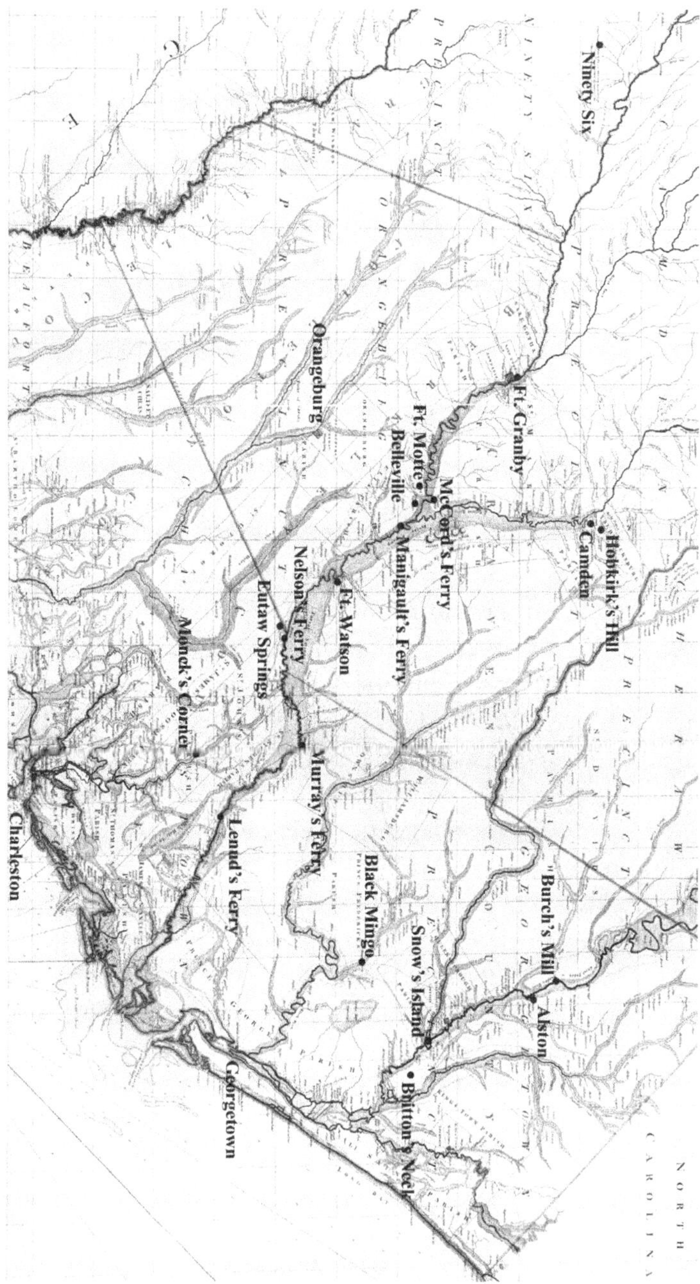

Figure 1. General Location of Marion and Lee's Campaign Against British Posts in 1781. (*William Faden 1780 Map adapted by John Fisher, Library of Congress*)

their attention on Marion and his Snow's Island partisans. First, in December of 1780, Major General Nathanael Greene reconstituted the remnants of the Continental Army in North Carolina.[5] Then in January 1781 the British suffered a setback. Lieutenant Colonel Banastre Tarleton's British Legion was severely whipped at the Battle of Cowpens by Brigadier General Daniel Morgan. The defeat alarmed Lord Charles Cornwallis, lieutenant general and commander of the British forces in the field, and he became obsessed with finding and catching both Morgan and Greene.[6] Burning his baggage wagons, he marched most of his forces northward into North Carolina, leaving the rest under the command of Lieutenant Colonel Francis Rawdon headquartered at Camden, South Carolina.[7] With the Southern Campaign of the American Revolution drawn into North Carolina, however, Rawdon had a free hand in South Carolina. Rawdon first concentrated on Thomas Sumter, forcing him into the backcountry of upper South Carolina.[8] Then Rawdon turned his full attention to the Swamp Fox and his community of partisans in and around Snow's Island, South Carolina.

Early in March, Rawdon ordered Lieutenant Colonel John W. T. Watson, camped at Fort Watson along the Santee River to find Marion and "press him to the utmost."[9] Shortly thereafter, Rawdon, acting on a tip from a Loyalist, set out a second punch, sending Lieutenant Colonel Welbore Ellis Doyle on his way toward Snow's Island from Camden.[10] Marion faced a two-pronged attack; though it is unclear if he knew that at the time. Either way, the result had been that the month of March had been a whirlwind of march, attack, retreat, and countermarch for Marion's partisans as he attempted to protect the Snow's Island community from Watson's force. Watson followed the Santee road eastward toward Snow's Island at the head of some five hundred men and two 3-pounder cannon.[11] Marion moved quickly to meet Watson and the two enemies met at a causeway through Wiboo Swamp. Watson's and Marion's forces traded attacks until eventually Marion retreated. This set up a series of repeated skirmishes as Watson attempted to force his way toward Snow's Island. Watson, however, would find Marion blocking his way at every river and creek crossing. The scenario played out several times. Watson would arrive at a river or creek crossing. After an exchange of gunfire, Watson would bring up his artillery to clear the way. Marion would then back off to await Watson at the next choke point. As he got closer to Snow's Island, Watson's casualties increased, and he became weaker and weaker from repeated harassment by Marion's men. Eventually, Watson's march to Snow's Island turned into a desperate rout simply to get to the safety of British held Georgetown. Marion stopped Watson, but meanwhile, Doyle marched on Marion's rear, found Marion's supply depot on Snow's Island, destroyed the camp, and made his way to Witherspoon's Ferry along Lynches Creek just west of Snow's Island.

With Watson in Georgetown, Marion turned north to find Doyle, sending his subordinate Peter Horry ahead. At Witherspoon's Ferry, crossing Lynches Creek, Horry and Doyle exchanged fire, but Doyle retreated up the river road along the west side of the Pee Dee and then turned away west toward Camden before Marion could catch up. The attempt to catch Doyle drew Marion all the way up the Pee Dee River to Joseph Burch's mill and plantation, some twelve miles north of Snow's Island. There he realized Doyle had gotten away leaving him with his Snow's Island depot destroyed, troop morale at a low point, and his community of partisans and supporters dispersed. There, in frustration, Marion had issued the proclamation.

Yet the British were not through. While Marion chased Doyle, Watson had refitted, rallied the local Loyalists, and with a great show marched north from Georgetown to meet and destroy Marion once and for all.

On that Thursday, Marion was down to three options—none good. He could attack the combined forces of Watson's regulars and Loyalist militia, some nine hundred men in all, with little possibility of success. He could attempt a dangerous recrossing of the Pee Dee exposed to a British attack. Or, as he discussed with his officers, he could disperse his troops and retreat to North Carolina, abandoning his loyal Snow's Island community. The latter tactic had worked once before. In September 1780, when British forces were about to surround him at Port's Ferry, he had retreated to White Marsh in North Carolina and hidden until able to return and surprise the British at Black Mingo.

With morale low, dispersal and retreat seemed the best option; then fortune smiled on Marion once again. Into the camp came a scout named Baker Johnson.[12] Johnson had seen Continentals upstream of the Pee Dee at Long Bluff. Shortly thereafter Captain James Conyers and a small party of Lieutenant Colonel "Light-Horse Harry" Lee's dragoons arrived confirming Johnson's intelligence. They reported that Nathanael Greene had returned to South Carolina and Lee was on his way to join Marion.[13]

This book details four short weeks, from April 12–May 12, 1781, in the partisan campaign of Francis Marion, from after the loss of his Snow's Island base of operations and the potential destruction of his forces, to his triumph, with the assistance of Henry Lee, in capturing Fort Motte, South Carolina.

Military historians writing grand histories of war focus on the great battles that changed the fortunes of war. Students studying the American Revolution learn about Trenton, Saratoga, and Yorktown. If one digs deeper, however, it is more often the small battles over time that make the difference. Such was what occurred in those brief four weeks during the Southern Campaign of the American Revolution. Over this short-lived period, American forces and fortunes in the South transitioned from a strategic defense to a relentless offense that would ultimately result in the British abandoning Charleston and South Carolina. Marion's role was also transformed—from an isolated partisan general barely holding the northeastern region of South Carolina, to Greene's reliable right fist. The capture of Fort Motte was a pivotal event in that transformation.

The road from Snow's Island to Fort Motte, however, was not straight. Before there was a Fort Motte, there was a Fort Watson and a Belleville, posts equally important to the security of the British Army's hold on the South Carolina backcountry, along with Fort Granby and Orangeburg. To completely dislodge the British, the Americans had to fight a "war of posts." To fully comprehend the significance of the capture of Fort Motte, we must understand how the fort came to be. It's a story that involves not only combatants, but also civilians caught up in war. Chapter 1 details Francis Marion's and Henry Lee's capture of Fort Watson, the first post to fall. Chapter 2 examines the broader strategic situation in South Carolina after the capture of Fort Watson and Marion's and Lee's road to Fort Motte. Chapter 3 steps back in time and relates the story of the Motte family, and especially a special lady named Rebecca Motte, who would build the mansion that became Fort Motte. Chapter 4 looks at the British road to Fort Motte. Chapters 5 and 6 detail the siege and its aftermath.

After the fall of Fort Motte, there would be many setbacks and losses yet to endure before American independence. The Southern Campaign, as it has been called in history, had another year and a half to go. Nevertheless, within these few weeks, the Americans fought the British to a standstill at Hobkirk's Hill, the British abandoned their backcountry stronghold at Camden, British supply depots at Forts Watson, Motte, Orangeburg, and Granby would fall in order, and Marion would go on to capture Georgetown soon after. Watson, Motte, and Georgetown were claimed by Marion. What follows is the story of Francis Marion's role in this critical phase of the American Revolution in South Carolina where small battles won the day.

ONE

The Siege and Capture of Fort Watson

PERHAPS, FOR A MOMENT, Lieutenant Colonel John W. T. Watson enjoyed a feeling of revenge and impending victory. He had invaded the Snow's Island region and scattered the Whigs after being battered by Marion along the Santee. His colleague in arms, Lieutenant Colonel Doyle, had destroyed Marion's depot on Snow's Island, and the Loyalist militia were pouring into Watson's camp, "and of a kind too, who when collected, even by themselves not the least afraid of Marion, would restore, if not quiet at least our Supremacy in that District."[1] Whatever joy he felt, however, was short-lived. Watson soon learned not only that Greene had returned, but that the Whig militia in Cheraw was assembling, and the most astonishing news—Lord Cornwallis "had quitted the Province," leaving the only large British force in the backcountry at Camden under Lieutenant Colonel Francis Rawdon.[2] With the road west to Camden blocked by Marion, and under the assumption that Marion and Lee would probably be assembling for an attack on Georgetown, Watson reversed his march and made for the coastal town. He took a different route back. Instead of recrossing the Pee Dee River at Britton's Ferry, he angled southeast and crossed the Little Pee Dee at Potato Bed Ferry. This route kept him closer to friendly Loyalist communities on the eastern banks of the Little Pee Dee, and after a fifty-mile march he arrived along the Waccamaw River on April 19.[3] As he marched southward, he experienced some of the frustration Marion had dealt with over the past year. The Loyalist militia melted away. Ironically, many of them returned to their homes and laid down their arms, just as Watson had ordered the rebellious Whigs to do in his proclamation when he had Marion trapped against the Pee Dee. Further, Watson's chasing Marion up the Pee Dee had accomplished very little strategically; he was desperately needed in Camden to reinforce Lord Rawdon, not stuck in Georgetown. Watson's excursion would deny Lord Rawdon the use of the 64th Regiment of Foot at the Battle of Hobkirk's Hill a few days later, as Watson would linger in Georgetown until late April. "The movements of Lt. Colonel Watson and *the unfortunate idea* of giving him the 64th Regiment *has been of more prejudice* that it is possible to describe, and it has not *only lost us* so very considerable *a force but* the troops *have been let down and the enemy of course* have gained much *ground* by it."[4]

Marion and Lee's commands joined forces on April 13 or 14, 1781, along the Santee, probably at Murray's Ferry.[5] The two officers were already acquainted, having joined forces in an attempt to take Georgetown, South Carolina, back in late January 1781. That endeavor failed, though they had demonstrated an ability to work in tandem. After Marion and Lee spent the evening catching up on the last few months, and after a debate as to what their objective should be, they marched to fulfill General Greene's order to "surprise" the British posts on the Santee River.[6] First on the list was Fort Watson, the British stronghold at Wright's Bluff on the east bank of the Santee River.

FORT WATSON

When the British captured Charleston in May 1780, they immediately deployed into the backcountry to occupy the villages and establish their authority. British or Loyalist detachments arrived at Orangeburg, Augusta, Ninety Six, Camden, Winnsboro, and Georgetown. Between these villages and Charleston, the British established small posts to rest and protect their supply trains. The primary route out of Charleston into the backcountry proceeded north to Monck's Corner where a post was established.[7] Troops could march to Monck's Corner or sail up the Cooper River to a landing and disembark. From there, troops and supplies proceeding to Ninety Six or Camden could take several routes north depending on their final destination. One main road ran north out of Monck's Corner to the Santee River where the road intersected the lower Santee road, paralleling the river and running east and northwest. If they were wanting to go to Camden or Ninety Six they could follow this lower Santee road along the west bank of the Santee northwest to where the road split, one branch turning east toward Camden where it crossed the Congaree River at McCord's Ferry. The other branch continued northwest to Ninety Six. Another option to travel to Camden was to cross the river a couple of miles north of the intersection of the lower Santee road with the Monck's Corner road at Nelson's Ferry, where the British constructed a redoubt. Once across the Santee and across the low, wide, Farrar Savannah, they would find the upper Santee road along the east or north bank of the Santee, which would lead north to Camden. Still another option was to march some six miles north of Nelson's to another ferry, where they could cross and join the upper Santee road.[8] Just north of that ferry, along the north or east bank, on top of a 1,200-year-old Indian mound, was Fort Watson, constructed in late December 1780, under the direction of Lieutenant Colonel John W. T. Watson.

Watson was a lieutenant colonel in command of a Provincial Light Infantry that was among a reinforcement of some 2,500 British soldiers arriving in Charleston in the middle of December 1780. Watson was unpopular among the British cadre and the commander of the British forces in the southern theater. Lieutenant General Charles Lord Cornwallis decided that it would be best for morale if Watson and his light infantry did not join the main army that winter. He expected there would be tension between Watson and Lieutenant Colonel Banastre Tarleton, who was more respected among the British cadre. Instead, Lieutenant Colonel Francis Lord Rawdon, commander of the British forces in Camden, agreed to take on "that plague" as Cornwallis described Watson. Under Rawdon, Watson was given the dubious honor of controlling the eastern region of South Carolina. Watson, for his part, painted the command a "distinguished situation." He welcomed the "detached command, the object of which was to protect the communications of the Santee River to Camden, and cover the Eastern District of the Province." The doorway to this region from Charleston was Nelson's Ferry and "that the eastern part of the Province was my front, that I was to consider Camden on the left, and George Town on the right as my flanks." The region was Francis Marion's home field. In other words, as of late December 1780, Francis Marion became Watson's problem . . . and good luck to him.[9]

Fort Watson was so placed to protect both the Santee crossings and as a forward operating base for operations to the northeastern part of the colony at what Watson described as a "weak point of the River."[10] A short distance away from the mound was Scott's Lake, a remnant oxbow once the main channel of the Santee River. The Indian mound was only 130 feet across and stood 23 feet above the surrounding landscape, 300 feet northwest of the old lake (Figures 2 and 3).[11]

The stockade consisted of a palisade, standing side-by-side vertical logs, secured in a foot-and-a-half-deep ditch, to create an enclosure measuring approximately fifty feet by fifty-five feet.[12] The sides were slightly offset from true north and not square, so that the southern and northern walls ran slightly northwest to southeast. Inside the fort, a couple of feet from the stockade wall, was a ditch that paralleled the walls on all four sides except at the fort's entrance.[13] This entrance, near the southeast corner, was

Figure 2. Fort Watson Mound. (*Courtesy Brian Mabelitini, 2017*)

twelve feet wide and faced slightly toward the southwest. There were also two other gaps in the stockade walls: one along the northern wall and another along the southwestern wall, both about two feet wide. These may have been for artillery and defended the fort from attack from the river. Watson had two 3-pounder cannons at the time of construction, but they would not be there during the siege. There also may have been a small interior structure in the fort's northeastern corner (Figure 4).

Watson most certainly had to reshape the mound for his use. He recorded that "we escarpt'd it at top, abattis'd [*sic*] it at the bottom and surrounded it as strong as the materials we could collect, and the only utensils we had, our tomahawks, would admit."[14] In other words, the top of the mound was leveled, and the sides shaved to form a smooth sloping plane to the base of the mound. Down the slope were arranged three rows of abatis and the land around the mound was cleared of trees.[15] The abatis consisted of either logs that were secured in the ground with pointed ends facing the enemy or simply cut trees piled side by side with their branches toward the enemy. At least one of the three rows of abatis consisted of logs rather than trees.[16] These abatis served to obstruct anyone from scaling the mound and attacking the fort.

In the clearing beyond the fort and mound the British encamped with tents and built a hospital and storage shed.[17] Most importantly for Marion and Lee, this camp contained many stores, supplies, and ammunition, including those that had been recently captured from Brigadier General Thomas Sumter of the South Carolina militia.[18]

Watson had left Lieutenant James McKay of the King's American Regiment in command of the fort, with thirty-six Loyalists of Major John Harrison's South Carolina Rangers and seventy-three British soldiers, when Watson began his campaign against Marion in March.[19] There were five other officers. There were also an unknown number of African Americans, most likely slaves from nearby plantations.[20]

THE SIEGE OF FORT WATSON

Around 4:00 p.m. on Sunday, April 15, Marion and Lee's men appeared at the edge of the eastern woods that surrounded the fort and camp.[21] The British immediately formed and fired at the intruders. More Americans poured out of the woods on McKay's left attempting to flank the British line.[22] Seeing the Americans emerging from the woods, McKay ordered a withdrawal into the fort. During the skirmish, a British private was mortally wounded. Both sides paused and regrouped.

Soon, Captain Carns of Lee's Legion appeared before the fort with a summons to surrender. McKay appeared at the gate and shouted down obstinately, "A British officer Commanded, & they timidly never surrendered Posts, if they wanted it, they must come to take it."[23] The Americans opened fire and the British answered. Another British soldier of the 64th Regiment of Foot was wounded, and McKay claimed that "several" Americans were seen to fall from the British return fire. As night fell, Marion and Lee deployed their command around the fort, sealing it from escape or resupply. Once dark, an American raiding party sallied out of

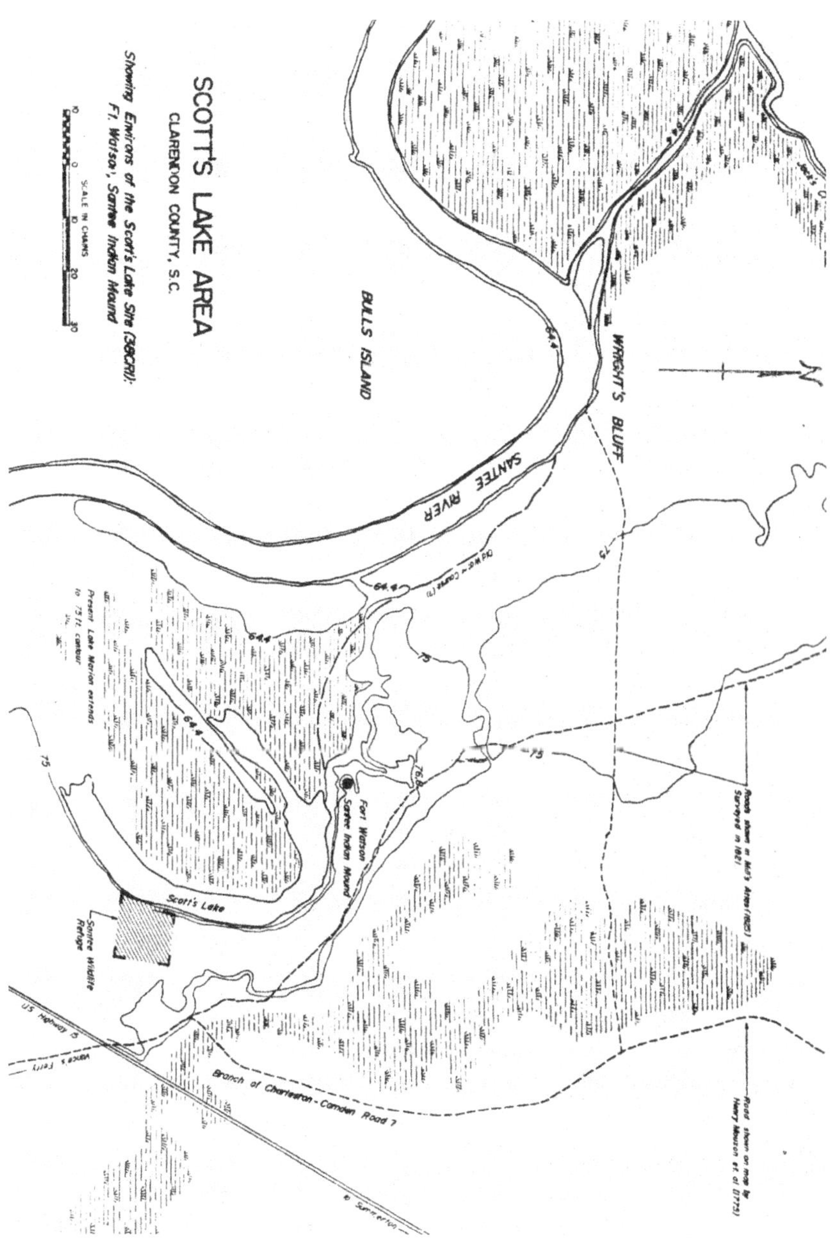

Figure 3. Fort Watson Environs Prior to Creation of Lake Marion. (*Ferguson 1975, courtesy SCIAA*)

the woods. Sick British soldiers and a nurse that had been left in the hospital were captured, dragged away, and the hospital was set on fire. In the chaos, a soldier in the 64th Regiment of Foot took advantage of the cover of darkness and deserted.

The next morning McKay assessed his situation. It was not good. One of the first things Marion had arranged that night was to place a detachment of riflemen and Lee's Continentals between the fort and the lake so that the fort's water supply was cut.[24] The British had had no time to collect water or food before retreating into the fort and had only whatever stores might have been in the fort prior to the attack. There was little to be done, as intermittent firing between the combatants continued through the day, keeping the British behind the walls. Two more British were wounded and "some" Americans were also.[25]

On Tuesday the intermittent firing continued and the situation inside the fort continued to deteriorate. Shots flew back and forth, and a private in Major John Harrison's Rangers was killed by a ball. Both sides eyed the abandoned supplies left on the field surrounding the fort. Yet neither side could safely get to the supplies while the sun was high. That night, though, under the cover of darkness, McKay decided to risk it. In the dark, a few British soldiers crept out of the fort and collected provisions, probably from a storehouse near the mound. Other soldiers boldly began digging a well just inside the abatis at the bottom of the hill.[26]

The advantage was not all to the Americans. By Wednesday, April 18, Marion and Lee realized the British were not going to meekly surrender. Yet, without artillery, all they could do was fire their rifles and muskets across the open space to keep the British heads below the stockade and wait them out. Throughout the day, the fire continued from both sides and the Americans lost a soldier. With mounting frustration, Marion and Lee realized it was becoming a stalemate. McKay would have agreed as he described it in his journal, the events of the last three days was a "blockade" rather than a siege.[27] Regardless, whatever it was called, the longer it continued the greater fortune would favor the British, despite being down to a half a pint of water daily for each man.

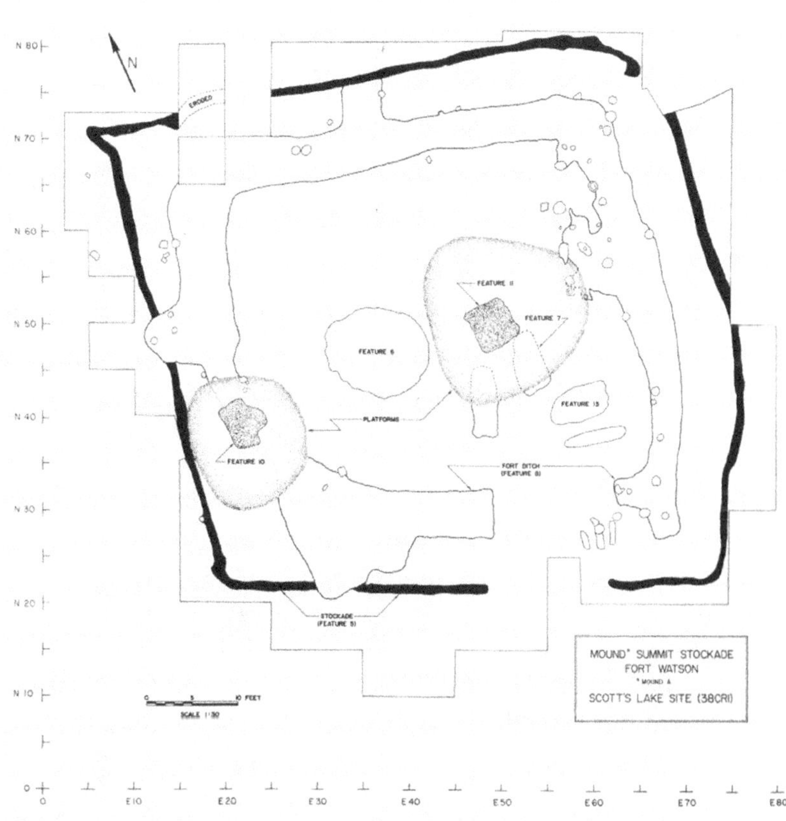

Figure 4. Fort Watson Excavation. (*Ferguson 1975, courtesy SCIAA*)

To break the deadlock, Lee wrote to General Nathanael Greene, who was north of Camden, South Carolina, and requested an artillery piece. Lee believed the cannon could get to them in a day and a half and would settle the matter in "five minutes."[28] Meanwhile, that night, both sides were busy. The British slinked out of the fort and gathered provisions, water, and most importantly, they found their rum. Nearby, oddly not running into the British sally, the Americans busily dragged off baggage that belonged to the 63rd and 64th Regiments. They also began digging entrenchments within one hundred yards of the fort.[29]

Thursday turned chaotic. Americans renewed firing at the fort and digging their entrenchments. At the same time, in defiance of American fire, the British worked on digging their well deeper at the base of the mound. Then suddenly, an American raiding party rushed out of the trees and began dragging off the remainder of the 63rd and 64th's baggage. British fire killed and wounded several. McKay, perhaps surprised to see provisions still outside the fort, ordered a raiding party of his own to gather any remaining provisions and water. Later, probably that night, two Loyalists escaped past Marion and Lee's guards and made for Nelson's Ferry to seek relief.

Meanwhile, behind the American lines, Lee got an unhappy reply to their request for a cannon. An artillery piece was not on its way. Greene felt he could not risk the trip as he did not have a sufficient surplus of men to safely escort the artillery around Camden and down to Fort Watson. He offered to release it if Lee could send an escort; however, he noted that he did not think the artillery would meet Marion and Lee's needs, suggesting the best way to take the fort was to cut off their water supply. Obviously, he had not been informed of the British well. Nevertheless, Greene was planning ahead, and asked if the artillery *could* be sent, could Lee and Marion get it across the Santee.[30]

Friday, the twentieth, British Corporal Shanks was killed by American fire. Undaunted, the British defied the Americans by constructing a covered way to their well. Meanwhile, they recovered three barrels of pork and four barrels of flour from the storehouse. While these provisions must have been welcome, it wasn't enough for Sergeant Brown, who deserted.[31] He took the garrison provision returns with him, perhaps as an offering to the Americans for his safety.

In the woods across the open field, frustration built as it was becoming clear that the Americans were unable to secure their blockade or keep the British from water and provisions near the fort. Lee's frustration was expressed in two letters written the same day, in which he reiterated the need for the artillery piece. "Nothing can be done by me without the desired aid: much may be done with it." This included crossing the Santee to support Greene's plan of reducing additional British posts. Adding to the overall precarious strategic situation, Marion, Lee, and Greene were worried about British Colonel Watson. Where was he? Was he marching toward Camden or perhaps toward them to relieve the fort? Lee noted that he and Marion would follow Watson if he moved, the implication being that they would have to lift the siege of Fort Watson.[32]

All the while Lee and Marion were attempting to take Fort Watson, an increasingly unhappy Marion was dealing with several command problems. There was an outbreak of smallpox in the American camp, resulting in more of Marion's men, who had not been inoculated, drifting away in the night. He received a rebuke from General William Moultrie, who had been in correspondence with the British commander in Charleston, Lieutenant Colonel Nisbet Balfour. Balfour had accused Marion's men of inflicting "many cruelties upon the people in the country, particularly in the murders of Mr. John Inglis, Capt. Clark, and John Frazee."[33] There is no indication that Marion attempted to defend himself against the charges and it appears that these "cruelties" occurred under the direct command of William Harden in the low country, who had been assigned to Marion's Brigade.[34] Then there was an insubordinate captain who was raising a command from Marion's recruiting grounds over along the Pee Dee River. Captain William Clay Snipes wanted a command of his own but did not want to serve under Marion. He had even interfered with Colonel Abel Kolb's attempts to raise men for Marion.[35] If all of the above were not frustrating enough, Marion's friend and colleague, Lieutenant Colonel Peter Horry, was feeling ill-used, writing Greene that he should be ranked senior to Lieutenant Colonel William Henderson.[36] This would be the beginning of Horry's discontent about his rank that later became a feud with another lieutenant colonel, Hezekiah Maham. All these issues were pressing on Marion's temper, which would eventually erupt in a couple of days.[37]

Despite these distractions, and a lack of men, Marion continued to make the most efficient use of his meager human resources. Marion's mounted detachments continued to patrol the Snow's Island region. A "small detachment" sent to watch the British at Camden captured a boat full of corn. He sent Colonel Hugh Horry to the Pee Dee to block Loyalists attempting to join Watson. They engaged a British foraging party.[38] On April 18, another of his officers, John James, provided thirty horsemen (a company), thirty horse provisions, and forage. On the twentieth Marion provided dinner for seventy men. The next day he provided dinner for twenty-eight men and on the twenty-fourth "Supper" for twenty men. Also noted is an unreadable entry but a few days later he added pork and twelve bushels of corn.[39] Most likely this detachment was camped at his plantation in northeastern Williamsburg Township. In the low country, Colonel William Harden had taken Fort Balfour, a fortified house at Pocotaligo, South Carolina.[40]

THE CAPTURE

The capture of the fort remained foremost in Marion's mind. From Marion and Lee's perspective, something different needed to be done to end the standoff once and for all. Major Hezekiah Maham offered a solution: build a log tower, which would allow the Americans to fire down into the fort. Sumter had used this ancient tactic in his failed attack on the British fortified post on the Congaree in February (see chapter 4).[41] Lee and Marion approved the plan. Maham got busy dispatching soldiers to nearby plantations to find axes and other tools to build the tower.

As usual, Saturday morning began with the American riflemen intermittently firing at the fort. One shot splintered the logs and wounded Lieutenant McKay in the face, and another hit a "negro" in the hand.[42] During the day, the Americans sent a flag to the fort, asking for a temporary cease-fire to gather and bury their dead still lying out in the open no man's land between the

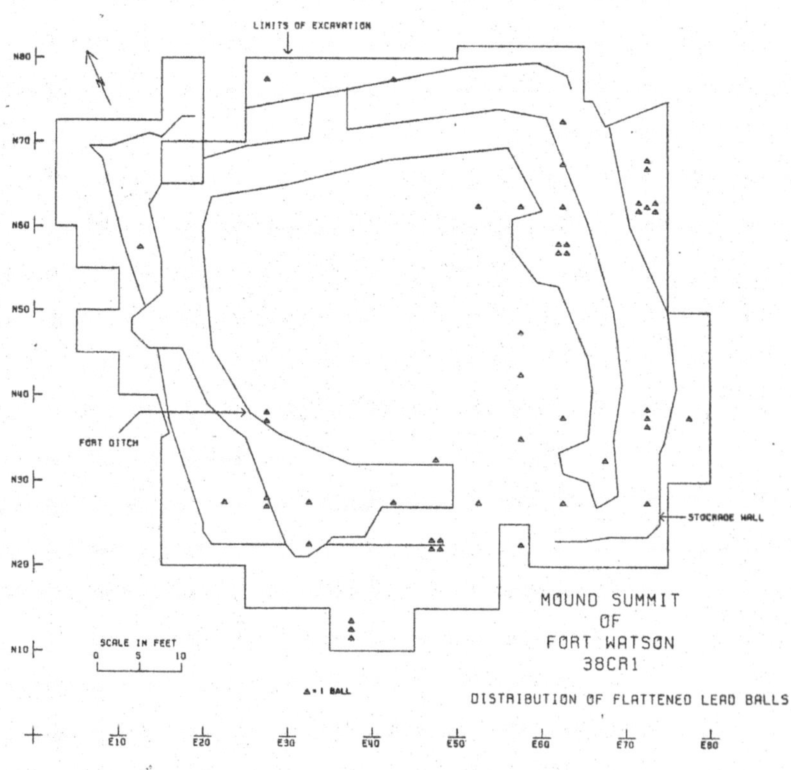

Figure 5. Distribution of Fired Lead Shot at Fort Watson. (*Ferguson 1975, courtesy SCIAA*)

fort and the wood line. McKay objected because the Americans would not agree to stop shooting.

Then, in the afternoon, the foundation of the tower was rolled up just next to the abatis at the base of the mound, near the northwest wall of the fort. Once in place, they continued to raise the height of the tower with additional logs high enough to fire down into the stockade (Figures 5 and 6). McKay immediately took measures to counter the tower by constructing a traverse across the middle of the fort and digging the interior ditches deeper. These ditches were dug a few feet from the fort walls all around the interior. He believed these two measures would allow

Figure 6. Artist's Conception of Maham Tower at Fort Watson. (*Darby Erd, courtesy SCIAA*)

the soldiers in the fort to hide from the American riflemen shooting at them from the tower.[43] Meanwhile, McKay's men, amazingly, were able to bring up more rum and water into the fort.

Sunday arrived as the siege entered its seventh day and the Americans continued their fire and worked on their tower. Colonel Lee, with increasing frustration, sent another flag to the fort offering a final opportunity to surrender. In his message, Lee reminded McKay of the British tactical situation. Exaggerating slightly, Lee stated that Camden was in the third day of a siege and Colonel Watson was not coming to rescue the British garrison. In reality, the Continentals under Greene were camped about a mile from Camden on Hobkirk's Hill and were in no way conducting a siege on Camden. Greene was focused on a rumor that Watson was marching toward Camden and the Americans. Actually, Watson was marching neither for Camden nor Fort Watson. In any case, Lee added in his message that there were Amer-

icans at the Congarees. In other words, McKay was isolated and without hope of rescue. Lee concluded with a vague threat that if McKay did not surrender immediately, Lee's subsequent conduct in the taking of the fort would be due to McKay's "obstinacy."[44] Lee gave McKay ten minutes to answer. McKay declined again, and the Americans opened new trench works outside the abatis near the well in an attempt to keep the British from bringing up more water. This did not work, but the British were forced to abandon their storehouse. McKay ordered a guard placed at the well to keep the Americans away. Another night passed. It would be the final.

On Monday, April 23, the blockade was in its eighth day and the Americans launched their attack. Riflemen climbed up the tower and began firing into the fort. Two British soldiers were killed, and McKay was wounded again. Jumping out of their trenches, a detachment of militia scrabbled forward to the outer abatis. Behind them came Lee's Legion infantry with fixed bayonets. At the first row of the abatis, the militia sappers began tearing away logs to open a passage. Two ensigns, Baker Johnson and "Mr. Lee," climbed up the mound and pulled down the abatis logs on the side of the hill, assisted by two lieutenants, McDonald and Coutirice.[45] Someone in the fort hung out a flag and again the British were summoned to surrender. McKay and his fellow officers were still full of fight, but the men in the fort grounded arms and refused to continue. McKay had no other option. Fort Watson was taken.[46]

The terms of surrender were generous and in keeping with the traditional honors of war in the eighteenth century. Lee did not make good on his threat and even complimented the "gallantry with which the post has been defended."[47] British officers were allowed to keep their arms and personal baggage. The British soldiers were disarmed and marched to Charleston to await exchange. The Loyalists were not treated as generously. They were made prisoners of war and sent to Hillsborough, North Carolina. In the end, 114 British enlisted and officers were captured, along with greatly needed ammunition and supplies.[48]

TWO

Searching for Watson

WHILE MARION AND LEE BESIEGED FORT WATSON, Major General Nathanael Greene, with the southern command of the Continental Army, was engaged in a standoff with British regulars occupying fortified Camden, South Carolina, under the command of Lieutenant Colonel Francis Lord Rawdon.

When Greene detached Lee to Marion, Greene was in North Carolina and began a march southward toward Camden, the keystone in the British arch of occupied villages in the South Carolina backcountry that included Augusta, Ninety Six, Camden, and Georgetown.[1] He arrived at Log Town, only a half mile north of Camden on April 19, 1781, the fifth day of Marion and Lee's siege of Fort Watson. Reconnoitering the Camden fortifications, he quickly decided that they were too strong to attack and retreated northward a few miles and encamped.[2]

Greene's appearance before Camden pressured Lord Rawdon who was on the frontier of British occupation in South Carolina, along with Ninety Six and Augusta. The intentions of Cornwallis, in Wilmington, North Carolina, were unknown to either one. Although Camden was a strong defensive position, many of Rawdon's men were ill. He needed the reinforcement of John Watson's detachment in Georgetown. For the next couple of weeks, Watson and Cornwallis would be on everyone's mind in South Carolina. Rawdon needed Watson in Camden and wondered if Cornwallis was going to return to South Carolina. Greene needed to keep both Watson and Cornwallis from joining Rawdon, and Marion and Lee were on the lookout.

Receiving intelligence that Watson was on the march, Greene circled eastward around Camden on April 21, detaching parties as he went searching for Watson. The intelligence proved false, and he quickly returned to the north side of Camden by the twenty-fourth, writing to Lee and Marion separately that the cannon Lee requested was finally on its way, along with powder and lead to make shot. Meanwhile, a small reinforcement of 130 South Carolina Royalists from Ninety Six had eluded Thomas Sumter and dashed into Camden to join Rawdon. With the whereabouts of Watson and Cornwallis unknown, Greene suggested that same day that Marion move north to join him before Camden.[3] The order came too late.

On April 25, 1781, Rawdon marched out of Camden and met Greene at Hobkirk's Hill, a gentle rise about a mile north of Camden. Rawdon had decided his best option was to attack, having heard from a deserter that Greene's artillery had been removed from Greene's camp at Hobkirk's Hill, and that Sumter, Lee, and Marion were on their way to join Greene.[4] The information about the artillery was true, but Greene had reversed the order and the cannon had arrived back in camp in time for battle. Although caught at breakfast, Greene's troops were in battle position and met Rawdon at the southeastern slope of the hill. As heavy firing began, Greene attempted a double envelopment and Rawdon countered by committing his reserves to extend his lines on both flanks. Meanwhile, in the center of the American line, the 1st Maryland Regiment under the command of Lieutenant Colonel John Gunby, for some reason, lost cohesion and retreated to reform, but by doing so, it spread panic along the American line, and Greene was forced to withdraw. Greene was furious but managed to extract his army and march north to Sanders Creek. Ultimately, no major harm was done. Generals and historians disagree on who won. Both sides had around 260 casualties. The British held the ground, but they had limited ability to reinforce, thus making their casualties more significant.[5]

After the fall of Fort Watson, Marion, with Lee's cavalry, moved north to William Richardson's Bloom Hill plantation in the High Hills of the Santee to be closer to Greene as ordered. Lee and the infantry soon joined. The day the battle raged on Hobkirk's Hill, Marion wrote to Greene with great apprehension, believing that Greene may have left the Camden region. He wrote that if he did not hear from Greene the following evening, he would make a sudden move to avoid any negative consequences as a result of Greene's absence.[6]

Greene finally replied on the twenty-sixth, congratulating Marion on the capture of Fort Watson and informing Marion of the previous day's battle. He again requested Marion to move north, but the following day he reversed that order, ultimately setting the stage for the siege of Fort Motte. After discussion with a Captain Conyers, Greene decided that Marion and Lee should go ahead with the previous plan to move against the British posts across the Santee.[7] Greene noted that if they crossed the river, they could take all the posts on the Congaree (Motte, Granby, Belleville, and perhaps even Orangeburg). Greene gave Marion free rein to act as circumstances permitted, going as far as an attack against Georgetown. Greene added that Captain Ebenezer Finley with a 6-pounder cannon and an escort of North Carolinians under Major Pinketham Eaton were, once again, on their way to Marion. Eaton, on the march to Marion, had heard about the fall of Fort Watson and decided to return to Greene, but Captain Conyers found them and turned them once more toward

Marion.[8] If Marion had known who made up Eaton's detachment, he might not have been all that impressed. Eaton commanded a reinforcement comprised of former militia who had deserted at the battle of Guilford Court House and were punished by being forced to serve a year in the Continental Army.[9]

Not having Greene's letter yet, Marion, on the twenty-seventh, was still anxious to learn Greene's whereabouts, writing that if Greene had indeed left, he and Lee were in a dangerous situation as Rawdon "was superior to us." Watson was still on everyone's mind and Marion's latest intelligence indicated that Watson had left Georgetown for Monck's Corner to collect another three hundred men before heading north.[10]

The letters flying back and forth between Greene, Marion, and Lee after Hobkirk's Hill perfectly reflect the fog of war. They lacked solid intelligence on the whereabouts of Cornwallis, Watson, and also Banastre Tarleton, who was operating with Cornwallis. These questions worried Marion to the point where he felt he needed to be on the move to avoid surprise. Thus, he first marched northward toward Greene and then, leaving a detachment at Rafting Creek, marched east to Salem, South Carolina, along the Black River.

From Salem he finally received Greene's letter and acknowledged the order to cross the Santee. Marion must have been thrilled: independent command and accompanied by Lee, with free rein to go as far as Georgetown! He noted that Watson must have been at Monck's Corner by that time and that if Tarleton was near Georgetown, Marion would try to intercept him.[11]

During these moves, Colonel Henry Lee and his legion remained close to Marion. On the twenty-seventh Lee wrote Greene, expressing the great opportunity afforded the Americans if, with reinforcements and the 6-pounder, he and Marion crossed the Santee to meet Watson and reduce the British posts.[12] He moved with Marion to Salem, and on the thirtieth informed Greene that they would first march for Benbow's Ferry, on the Black River, then cross the Santee at Fort Watson, and let the most recent intelligence determine if they should turn south to find Watson, or north toward Fort Motte.[13]

At about this time, April 28, Marion received word that Colonel Abel Kolb had been surrounded at his home and had been shot and killed attempting to surrender. Kolb had been an active and effective, perhaps ruthless, militia officer operating under Marion in the Pee Dee upcountry. In the vicious civil war between Loyalists and Patriots, Kolb was known to retaliate against Loyalists for hangings and ambushes, with his own. Kolb defended his family and home, killing several Loyalists, before they threatened to burn the house. Kolb agreed to surrender but was then shot and his house burned. Marion detached John Ervin to find the murderers and punish them, but Ervin never caught up to them.[14]

On the second of May, Marion and Lee were at Benbow's Ferry, where Eaton, his escort, and critically, the 6-pounder cannon finally joined them.[15] No doubt they were exhausted, having marched and countermarched as Marion and Greene decided their fate. The now powerful detachment of militia, Continentals, and a cannon proceeded to Fort Watson and crossed over the Santee to the west bank. They missed Watson by a day, perhaps only hours.[16]

Watson had finally left Georgetown on his march to reinforce Rawdon. Under orders from the British commander in Charleston, Nisbet Balfour, he lingered at Lenud's Ferry on the Santee for a couple of days, waiting to see if Cornwallis or Tarleton were coming back to South Carolina. From there he proceeded to Monck's Corner, picking up additional men, and then began his march along the western road toward Camden, passing Nelson's Ferry and the ferry that Marion and Lee crossed later that very night. He could have gone to Fort Motte and crossed the Congaree at McCord's Ferry, but concerned about being spotted by either Marion's or Sumter's scouts, he crossed at an unguarded, rarely used, ferry just below the confluence of the Wateree and the Congaree called Buchenham's (Buckingham's) Ferry on May 5, thus eluding Sumter, Marion, and Marion's detachment at Rafting Creek. After a difficult march, which included crossing swollen creeks and constructing a road, he arrived in Camden on May 7.[17]

Watson, having eluded Marion and Lee, was now accounted for. He had dodged Marion and Lee and reinforced Rawdon. Cornwallis and Tarleton, however, were still missing. Correspondence between Greene, Marion, Lee, and Sumter continued to reflect their worry about Cornwallis's possible return to South Carolina. Their concerns were unfounded. Cornwallis was in Wilmington, North Carolina, trying to convince himself of the value of going north to Virginia rather than returning to South Carolina. As early as the tenth of April he had written to British Major General William Phillips in Virginia that he was considering a junction. He argued that "marching about in quest of adventures" in the Carolinas would not work and believed that moving the entire British force in New York to Virginia would allow for offensive action and "have a stake to fight for."[18] Meanwhile, as late as April 22, he was writing to Balfour in Charleston that he could not decide whether to enter South Carolina through Georgetown or the head of the Waccamaw River.[19] Virginia, however, was probably his desire all along, and on the day Rawdon would march out of Camden, May 10, Cornwallis began his march north to his fate in Virginia. Tarleton, who had spent most of his time recuperating from a battle wound in Wilmington, was ordered to the Cape Fear River to assist in locating boats to cross.

After Hobkirk's Hill, Greene retreated to Sanders Creek, then further north to Rugeley's plantation, passing through the old Camden battlefield eight miles from the town. He crossed the Wateree and arrived at 25 Mile Creek on May 4. Rawdon, meanwhile, was contemplating his own situation, and it was becoming increasingly precarious from his perspective. Watson's arrival was good news, but his troops were exhausted from their march. Watson informed Rawdon that Fort Watson had fallen, and soon after he learned that Marion and Lee were before Fort Motte. Nevertheless, Rawdon felt he had to at least make one more attempt to throw off Greene and the evening of May 7, he crossed the Wateree and marched for Greene. He found Greene on a high, well protected ridge along Sawney's Creek. There was no possibility of success against Greene in that position, so Rawdon did an about-face and returned to Camden on the afternoon of the eighth. The next day, he posted orders for the evacuation of Camden.[20]

Meanwhile, Greene had had a moment of panic. He had written to both Marion and Lee on May 4 that he thought Cornwallis was coming from Wilmington. He ordered Lee to join him with the artillery piece and asked Marion how many of his men he thought would join the Continentals if needed.[21] Lee and Marion, however, had already crossed the Santee and had marched for Fort Motte. In fact, Greene's recall letter to Lee reached Lee only "a few moments" after their arrival before the fort.[22] News quickly reached Lee and Marion that all was well, and the siege began.

THREE

The Mottes and Mount Joseph

AT THE VERY BEGINNING OF THE AMERICAN REVOLUTION, wealthy Charleston merchant, Miles Brewton II, owned a plantation along the Congaree River that he named Mount Joseph. It would become, during the American Revolution, the location of Fort Motte. Miles was born into the prominent Brewton family that had come to South Carolina in the 1680s from Barbados. Like his father before him, Miles became engaged in a variety of mercantile businesses. He was part owner of as many as eight ships and eventually became "South Carolina's largest slave dealer," and "one of the wealthiest men in the province."[1] Like many colonial entrepreneurs, he had his hands in numerous business and land interests. During his life, he purchased several tracts of land in South Carolina totaling over twelve thousand acres, including Mount Joseph, which he purchased 1772.[2] He married Mary

Izard, further increasing his business ties and fortune. In 1765, he began the construction of his lavish and still-standing Brewton house, on King Street in Charleston. He was also a member of the Commons House of Assembly and the Council of Safety. He was elected to the second Provincial Congress in August 1775, and was on his way to Philadelphia when he, his wife, and children were lost at sea.[3]

Miles Brewton grew up in a blended family, his father Robert having been married twice. One of his half-sisters was Rebecca, born June 15, 1737. She was the fourth of five children in Robert Brewton's family. She was to the manor born, part of a prominent family, and connected through marriages to many prominent business, military, and political figures in mid-eighteenth-century Charleston. In the eighteenth century, death often came early from a variety of illnesses and accidents, and by the time Rebecca was eighteen, she had lost two sisters, and only Miles and sister Frances were living.[4] On June 11, 1758, Rebecca married Jacob Motte Jr.

Jacob Motte was also a prominent plantation owner and politician. His family, like Francis Marion's, were Huguenots. They came to Charleston in the early 1700s. By the time Jacob and Rebecca were married, the Mottes were also part of the wealthy Charleston elite. His father, Jacob Sr., had lost most of his business in a great fire that swept through Charleston in 1740, but had been able to recover much of this wealth when he was elected public treasurer in 1743. Then a hurricane struck, again destroying the family business and Jacob Sr. had to declare bankruptcy.[5] These tragedies did not spoil the family name and Jacob Jr. still mixed with the upper crust in Charleston and eventually noticed Rebecca Brewton, who was a neighbor, and they were married. The following year, his father was able to pay off his debts and was restored his property. Jacob Jr. would profit from his father's fame and fortune and garner his own. During his life he served several times in the Royal Assemblies between 1760 and 1775. He also served in the Second Provincial Congress, and the First, Second, and Third General Assemblies between 1775 and 1780.[6]

Jacob and Rebecca settled in Charleston and purchased Fairfield Plantation on the lower Santee River in 1758.[7] Jacob was justice of the peace of St. James Santee Parish in 1767 so it's likely they had moved to Fairfield by then, but still splitting their time between Charleston where Jacob's business interests continued, and their Fairfield Plantation.[8]

The Mottes were ardent supporters of the American cause. Throughout the war they supplied South Carolina's soldiers with rice, beef, pork, corn, and fodder. After the war, Rebecca was awarded over six hundred pounds sterling for provisions she supplied the troops from 1778 through 1783.[9] Rebecca's role, however, would overshadow Jacob's contributions as she became an icon of the American Revolution as a result of her ownership of Mount Joseph.

That story begins with the death of Miles Brewton at sea in 1775. Eventually, his ship was reported missing, and Rebecca Brewton Motte and her sister Frances realized they were the inheritors of a large estate including the Brewton House in Charleston and Mount Joseph Plantation. By some agreement, Rebecca, her husband Jacob, and their three daughters moved into the Charleston home. The sisters also agreed in 1777 to split two of Miles's plantations along the Congaree River. On September 9, Frances obtained full ownership of Greenwich and Rebecca obtained full ownership of Mount Joseph.[10]

By this time, Jacob and Rebecca's oldest daughter Betsey was in her late teens and had the attention of Thomas Pinckney. He had noticed Betsey as early as 1775 when she was only thirteen and the interest had grown until they married on July 22, 1779.[11]

At the time of their marriage, Thomas Pinckney was a Major in the 1st South Carolina Regiment. Born into another prominent South Carolina colonial family, Pinckney had spent much of his teens in England, attending Westminster School at age thirteen, and later Christ Church Oxford. He came home briefly in 1771 but returned in 1773 to finish his legal studies. By 1775, he was back in South Carolina assisting in the construction of fortifications around Charleston Harbor, where, on James Island he watched the British bombardment of Fort Moultrie across the bay in 1776.[12] An active recruiter, Thomas took a recruiting trip all the way to Baltimore, Maryland, in 1777. In 1779, the British burned Auckland, his Ashepoo River home, and that same year he was second in command of the front line at the battle of Stono River—where he may or may not have known that his old school friend, Captain Charles Barrington McKenzie of the 71st Highlanders, fought against him.[13] They were destined to meet on the battlefield again.

When the British besieged Charleston beginning in March 1780, Rebecca Motte offered her slaves to American general Benjamin Lincoln to assist in constructing defenses.[14] When the British occupied Charleston in May, the Brewton House was seized and used as a headquarters. For a while Rebecca remained in the house and tradition has it that she used her female slaves to slip messages about British activities in Charleston to Francis Marion.[15] There is every reason to believe this occurred. Rebecca was a well-known and respected member of Charleston society. Both were Santee plantation owners. Marion had been in and around Charleston as a soldier since 1775 when he represented St. John's Parish at the first meeting of the Provincial Congress.[16] It's reasonable to assume Mrs. Motte and Marion were acquainted and were able to set up an intelligence system.

Other stories of Rebecca in Charleston after the siege include the British occupation of her inherited home there. British officers occupied the house, including General Henry Clinton and Colonel Francis Rawdon. Rebecca kept her daughters in the garret away from the officers.[17] Despite these stories, historian Margaret Pickett asserts that the Mottes had left Charleston in April before the fall of Charleston the following May.[18] According to Pickett, the Mottes moved to Fairfield Plantation including Rebecca, Jacob, daughters Fanny, Mary, and pregnant Betsey Pinckney, along with Jacob's sister, Martha Motte Dart, Dart's children, and Rebecca's niece Mary "Polly" Brewton.[19] Whenever they left, the Mottes were probably not in Charleston on May 12, 1780, when American forces surrendered. Neither was Major Pinckney, who had been ordered out of Charleston at the end of April, to deliver a message to the rebel governor of South Carolina, John Rutledge.[20]

Pinckney heard the news of the surrender and hurried to Fairfield to visit his wife and in-laws. Sometime after May 18, British colonel Banastre Tarleton raided Fairfield in the middle of the night. Thomas Pinckney was able to escape, but Jacob Motte possibly was captured. At least this is the most likely outcome, since shortly afterward, Rebecca and the rest of the family moved to Mount Joseph on the Congaree River.[21]

MOUNT JOSEPH PLANTATION

The main portion of Mount Joseph Plantation is located on two high bluffs overlooking the Congaree River around a mile upstream from where the Congaree and Wateree drained into the Santee. At the time of the revolution, a large, sharp bend in the river took its course nearly a mile east before bending back west, almost on itself, before turning sharply southeast and downstream to meet the Wateree. This oxbow bend was breached during a massive flood in the 1850s. McCord's Ferry was at the very eastern turn of the river and Buckhead Creek was at the downstream bend. The two high Congaree River bluffs were separated by a wide, deep ravine, over one hundred feet deep, and the eastern bluff was called Buckhead Hill. Buckhead Creek, where the Congaree turned southeast, also created a deep ravine, and isolated the two Congaree bluffs from another one to the southeast, separating Mount Joseph from Colonel William Thomson's Belleville Plantation (Figures 7 and 8).[22]

There are few extant records providing clues to the plantation's development and use prior to the war. As noted, Rebecca Motte gained ownership upon Miles Brewton's death. Brewton had acquired Mount Joseph from Benjamin Farrar for 2,500 pounds on July 11, 1772.[23] Miles Brewton's will indicates that Mount Joseph Plantation consisted of 1,300 acres. The deed between Farrar and Brewton indicates only 1,000 acres, however, at the time of sale. Four hundred acres were on the south or west

Figure 7. Fort Motte, Belleville, and McCord's Ferry Environs. (*William Faden Map 1780, adapted by John Fisher, Library of Congress*)

side of the river, and 600 acres of swampland "opposite first tract."[24] Sometime after 1772, Brewton acquired the additional 300 acres. Coincidentally, according to Brewton's deed, the 400 acres on the south side of the river once had been part of a tract of land granted to Job Marion, Francis Marion's brother. Another intriguing connection between the Motte and Marion families.

There is almost no firm information about the improvements to the plantation prior to Rebecca's ownership. The deed between Brewton and Farrar states that Brewton acquired the land and all gardens, orchards, fences, ways, water courses, and wells on the property.[25] While this indicates some improvements, there is no mention of structures. Brewton's will, which left the plantation to his wife, indicates that she, ultimately Rebecca, would inherit "all my stock of cattle, horses, & other stock and plantation tools and utensils at my Mount Joseph Plantation on the Congaree River."[26] No doubt some unknown numbers of slaves were already there, and an overseer, likely working the cattle and horses, as a cattle farm. The plantation might also have grown indigo in the swampland across the river. Belleville Plantation, next door, was an indigo plantation.[27]

When the Mottes arrived, they must have moved into the overseer's house on Buckhead Hill described as a "farm house or "old log cabin."[28] This house is likely to have been formerly owned by the Lloyd family, depicted on Mouzon's 1775 map of South Carolina.[29] Archaeological excavations indicate that the house was likely very small and rustic, and built on wooden or stone piers.

The Mottes arrived in early June after a difficult float up the Santee and Congaree Rivers. A letter from Eliza Lucas Pinckney to Betsey Motte dated June 18, 1780, notes that "it gave us great concern to hear of the frights and hardships you underwent in your journey and continuance of them since you have been up, the disappointment in your boat must have render'd your situation most uncomfortable."[30]

One situation that quite likely increased their frights and hardships was, upon arrival, to find the British occupying their neighbor's plantation. They had moved to avoid British intrusion at Fairfield only to find them about a mile away at Belleville.

THE MOTTES AND THOMAS PINCKNEY

The Mottes at Buckhead would spend the summer and fall of 1780 dealing with sickness and British harassment. "Fevers" began in July and "attacked our Children and Negroes early." Eliza Pinckney had suggested they get inoculated against smallpox the previous month and Betsey acknowledged its importance as, "it will be almost impossible for our family to Escape, as it is in every plantation within 15 miles." Meanwhile, "The Army has taken all our provisions" so the Mottes sent their remaining horses downstream via their slave Samson.[31] Betsey gave birth to a son in Au-

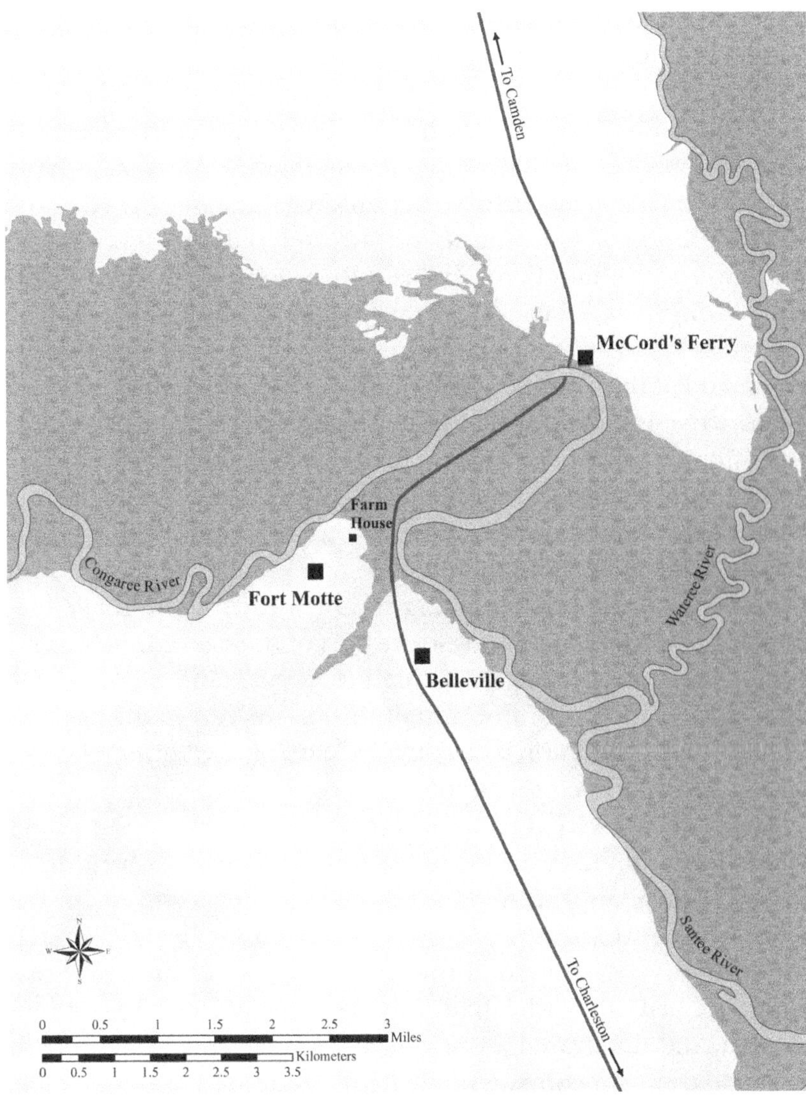

Figure 8. Fort Motte, Belleville, and the Old Farmhouse. (*Tamara Wilson, courtesy SCIAA*)

gust and later that month her husband, Thomas Pinckney, was severely wounded at the battle of Camden, August 16, 1780.

Pinckney had made his way to Camden after the raid at Fairfield Plantation. From there he journeyed into North Carolina and joined Baron de Kalb and a detachment of Maryland Continentals who had been enroute to reinforce the Americans defending Charleston. When Charleston surrendered, de Kalb stopped his march at Buffalo Ford on Deep River to await further orders from Congress. Against General George Washington's wishes, Congress placed General Horatio Gates, the hero of Saratoga, in command of the Continental Army in the Southern theater. When Gates arrived at camp and took command on July 25, 1780, Pinckney offered his services and was made an aide to Gates.[32]

The fate of Gates's army is a well-known story. With Virginia and North Carolina militia expected to join Gates and swell his army to some four thousand men, he quickly marched into South Carolina with the goal of taking the British stronghold at Camden. Gates chose the most desolate part of the backcountry as his route. The men became ill eating green corn and peaches, the only food available, but eventually, the army reached Rugeley's Mill, thirteen miles north of Camden. On August 14, the Virginia militia finally arrived to complete his command.

Gates decided Rugeley's was indefensible and wanted to get closer to Camden. A hillside with a creek in front, seven miles from Camden, appeared to be a more strategic position. On the night of August 15, at ten o'clock, Gates's army began a march south along a narrow road toward the hill and Camden. Lord Charles Cornwallis, who had only recently arrived in Camden, also saw the disadvantages of Gates's camp and marched north to surprise Gates, coincidentally leaving Camden at ten o'clock. The two forces met at two o'clock in the morning in a deep but open pine virgin forest with a tall grass understory. After a brief skirmish, both sides fell back and prepared for what was going to be a major battle at dawn.

Gates aligned his forces in the conventional manner with his best troops, the Continentals, on his right, west of the road, and his militia on the left, east of the road. In reserve was the 1st Maryland Brigade, which had become disorganized in the night skirmish. Cornwallis let his men rest along the road and when dawn broke, he followed Gates's deployment, placing his regulars on the right, east of the road, and his Provincials on the left or west side. This placed Cornwallis's best units against Gates's untested militia. Cornwallis's reserve consisted of the 71st Highlanders and Tarleton's dragoons, all veterans of many battles.

As dawn broke, Cornwallis's regulars were seen deploying and the battle opened with Gates's artillery firing canister into their ranks. Undaunted, the British regulars charged Gates's militia, who immediately fled, many without firing a shot. The Marylanders in reserve opened its ranks to let them pour through. Then they marched forward to engage the British while on the opposite side of the road, the battle was hotly engaged, the action engulfed in gun smoke from musket and artillery fire. Two battles were being fought, and Cornwallis saw his opportunity as the gap between the battles on the left and right grew wider. He sent Tarleton's cavalry and the 71st into the gap. Gates's army was crushed. Tarleton's dragoons chased the militia twenty-two miles up the road to Hanging Rock. Perhaps as many as 800 Americans were killed and wounded, and 700 prisoners taken. The British lost 68 killed, 245 wounded, and 11 missing.

Pinckney was one of the American wounded. Under normal circumstances, Betsey was very likely to have become a widow. He was, however, found on the battlefield with a shattered left leg by Major Charles McGill, placed in a wagon, and taken back up the road toward Rugeley's. At the bridge across Grannies Quarter Creek, he was carried across because the "causeway" was blocked by wagons and then placed in a baggage wagon. Then, none other than Captain Charles Barrington McKenzie of the 71st Highlanders, his school chum, found him unconscious. Tarleton's surgeon was called, and he field dressed Pinckney's wound and set the wagon for Camden. On the way, he passed through the battlefield where he heard the "groans of many," including one Continental who begged to be taken in the wagon.

He was picked up but was later turned out for a British soldier by the wagoner, who damned Pinckney when he protested. Pinckney was taken to the home of Ann Clay and, according to tradition, refused to wake up Mrs. Clay since it was late in the evening and the lights were out.[33]

McKenzie and the British command continued to assist in Pinckney's immediate care. Indeed, Pinckney wrote General Gates only two days after the battle, that "I received every Mark of kindness and Attention, I am likewise under great Obligation to the Officers in General & Gentlemen of the Faculty for their Civility and Care of me."[34] McKenzie requested, and Colonel Banastre Tarleton agreed, to have Tarleton's surgeon continue to look after the major.[35]

Indeed, the relationship between the Mount Joseph clan and the British over the fall and winter was a mixed bag. The British seized horses and supplies, and probably slaves, but British officers would stop in on their way to and from Charleston, dropping off letters between the Pinckneys and Mottes. Even Tarleton got involved in this gentlemanly relationship, attempting to recover the Mottes' horses that had been taken by the British during the summer. Given that good cavalry horses were in high demand by both sides, this was quite remarkable.[36] An example of how Mount Joseph became a nearly routine stopover for the British, even while they occupied Belleville, is seen in a letter Pinckney wrote to his sister Harriott Pinckney Horry in Charleston on September 7, 1780, in which he requests port wine and bark as an aid to his healing. He notes that if she can get it to Mount Joseph, he can have it forwarded to Camden.[37] This friendly interaction between foes extended to Belleville. In another letter between Harriott Pinckney Horry in Charleston and Thomas Pinckney in Camden, Harriott explains that Colonel Thomson, on parole at Belleville, was sending a wagon down to Charleston and that she will send some wine to the Mottes via the wagon when it returns to Belleville.[38] In that same letter, she notes that a Captain Coffin had just stopped by to pick up letters to Tom before heading for Camden. Coffin did not spend any time at Camden, as he returned to Charleston, with letters from Tom, sometime before September 17. On his way down, he stopped at the Mottes'.[39]

Through early September, Pinckney, working through British Major John Money, requested permission to go to Mount Joseph where his wife and a local surgeon could assist in his recovery. Once recovered he promised to report to Orangeburg while awaiting an exchange. Lord Cornwallis granted permission on September 24.[40] Betsey was too weak to go to Camden, so in her stead went Jacob Motte (who was quite possibly also a parolee) and a doctor. He placed Pinckney in a periagua (canoe) and brought him to Mount Joseph via the Wateree and Congaree Rivers. He was there by October 13.[41]

MOUNT JOSEPH, NOVEMBER 1780–MAY 1781

At Mount Joseph, Thomas Pinckney learned more about the difficulties Betsey and the family at Mount Joseph had in August and September. Illnesses had continued through the summer months and tragedies plagued the household through the fall. Little Benjamin Dart, Rebecca's nephew, died from eating too many "ground nuts."[42] In November, smallpox, which had been around throughout the neighborhood, finally arrived at Mount Joseph. Thomas Pinckney and Rebecca were immune, but Betsey and child both caught the disease; yet they survived and were in recovery by December. Sometime late that month or early December, Rebecca Motte lost her three-year-old daughter Becky.[43] This tragedy was followed by another sometime in late January when Mr. Jacob Motte disappeared. There is no record of him dying, and no letters mentioning his death. He simply disappeared. The last mention of him is in a letter from Harriott Pinckney Horry to Eliza Lucas Pinckney on January 7, 1780, the context of which suggests he was still alive. Historian Margaret Pickett believes he embarked on a trip to Charleston around December 6, based on a letter from Thomas Pinckney to his mother Eliza Lucas Pinckney, in which Jacob Motte is to "convey" Pinckney's situation concerning his health to Eliza.[44] A monument to him at St. Philip's Episcopal Church indicates he died on January

20, 1781.[45] No letters describe his death and oddly, Thomas Pinckney and Betsey traveled to Charleston at about this same time as his leg was not getting better. They were in Charleston by January 15.[46]

Thomas Pinckney's wound would eventually heal, and he and Betsey would travel to Germantown, near Philadelphia, Pennsylvania, still a POW awaiting an exchange. He returned to South Carolina in January 1782, even stopping on the way south to visit Horatio Gates at his plantation home.[47]

Events at Mount Joseph from January to the beginning of the siege of Fort Motte on May 6 are not well-known. Rebecca must have been in deep mourning having lost her daughter and her husband. Perhaps the only bright spot in her life was that her new mansion, which probably had been under construction for a few months, was finally finished. She could move in with her remaining family of four women and four or five children.[48] Alas, so did the British.

Henry Lee, by James Herring, c. 1834. Nathanael Greene detached Lieutenant Colonel Henry Lee and his legion to join Francis Marion in the captures of Fort Watson and Fort Motte. (*National Portrait Gallery*)

Rebecca Motte, by Jeremiah Theus, c. 1758. The Widow Rebecca Brewton Motte was a wealthy landowner and supporter of the American rebellion, her newly built Mount Joseph mansion was fortified by the British in 1781, becoming Fort Motte. (*Metropolitan Museum of Art*)

Thomas Sumter, by William Armstrong, c. 1835. Sumter was commander of the South Carolina militia at the captures of Fort Watson and Fort Motte; he made attempts to capture Fort Granby and Thomson's Plantation, and eventually captured the British post at Orangeburg. (*National Portrait Gallery*)

Francis Rawdon, by Martin Archer Stone. Lieutenant Colonel Francis Rawdon was left in command of British field forces in South Carolina when General Charles Cornwallis moved into North Carolina early in 1781. (*Wikimedia Commons*)

Nathanael Greene, by Charles Wilson Peale, 1783. Major General Greene took command of the Continental forces in the Southern Theatre in December 1781 and remained in that position until the end of the war. (*Independence National Historical Park*)

Thomas Pinckney, by W. C. Armstrong, after John Trumbull. The husband of Betsey Motte, Thomas Pinckney was an aide to General Horatio Gates, wounded at the battle of Camden, and recovered at Rebecca Motte's plantation in the fall of 1780. (*New York Public Library*)

Francis Marion, the "Swamp Fox," was a partisan commander in the northeast part of South Carolina who teamed up with Henry Lee to capture Fort Watson and Fort Motte. (*New York Public Library*)

Placed in command of British forces in the Southern Theatre after the capture of Charleston, South Carolina, in 1780, Charles Cornwallis would eventually surrender his army at Yorktown, Virginia. (*New York Public Library*)

FOUR

British in the Neighborhood

WHEN THE BRITISH MOVED INTO THE BACKCOUNTRY after the fall of Charleston in May 1780, they immediately occupied the villages of Camden, Augusta, Ninety Six, and Georgetown. Marching to Camden, they could take the road out of Monck's Corner that crossed the Santee River near Eutaw Springs at Nelson's Ferry and travel up the eastern side of the Santee, or they could follow the southern or western road along the Santee and cross the Congaree at McCord's Ferry. Cornwallis, on his way to Camden shortly after the capture of Charleston, chose the eastern road. Colonel Nisbet Balfour, on his way to Ninety Six, chose the western road. Both routes required stopping and encamping at various plantations, and eventually the more often used plantations at important locations were fortified. Near McCord's Ferry along the western route, the British chose Belleville, the home of Colonel William Thomson (Figure 9).

THE BRITISH OCCUPY BELLEVILLE

Thomson, whose nickname was "Old Danger," was a popular and prominent plantation owner in the region, and prior to the war was in and out of political office. As mentioned, his plantation was adjacent to Buckhead and about a mile away from the hilltop where Rebecca Motte would build her Mount Joseph Plantation mansion. Thomson had joined the rebellion early in the war and had taken part in the 1775 Snow Campaign into the backcountry Ninety Six District, which blunted Loyalist opposition there. He was also at the battle of Fort Sullivan in June of 1776 when a British expedition attacked the fort on Sullivan's Island, South Carolina. There he commanded the blocking force that stopped a British landing party attempting to cross onto the island and flank the fort. He was made a colonel in the 3rd South Carolina Regiment. In 1778, he resigned his commission but was in command of the Orangeburg Patriot militia when the British besieged Charleston.[1]

British Lieutenant Colonel Nisbet Balfour, marching for Ninety Six, arrived at Thomson's on June 6, 1780, in command of some six hundred men, including three companies of the 7th Regiment Royal Fusiliers, light infantry, the Prince of Wales American Regiment, and Major Patrick Ferguson with his American Volunteers.[2] Ninety Six was some one hundred miles to the northwest and Belleville was a good place to stop and rest, but Balfour also had intelligence that there were flour and stores at the plantation that had not yet been confiscated.[3] On inspection he found "some Indian flour with nearly a puncheon of rum, some cattle, and other trifling objects." He also found William Thomson and his teenage son, William Russell Thomson, who were captured.[4] The detachment spent three more days at Thomson's from June 7 to June 10, and then continued their march northward to Ninety Six via the Congarees near modern-day Columbia, leaving two flank companies of the Prince of Wales American Regiment under Major Colin Graham, along with the sick, all amounting to around one hundred men.[5]

Occupying Belleville sent a message to the regional population, symbolizing that those who took up arms against the King

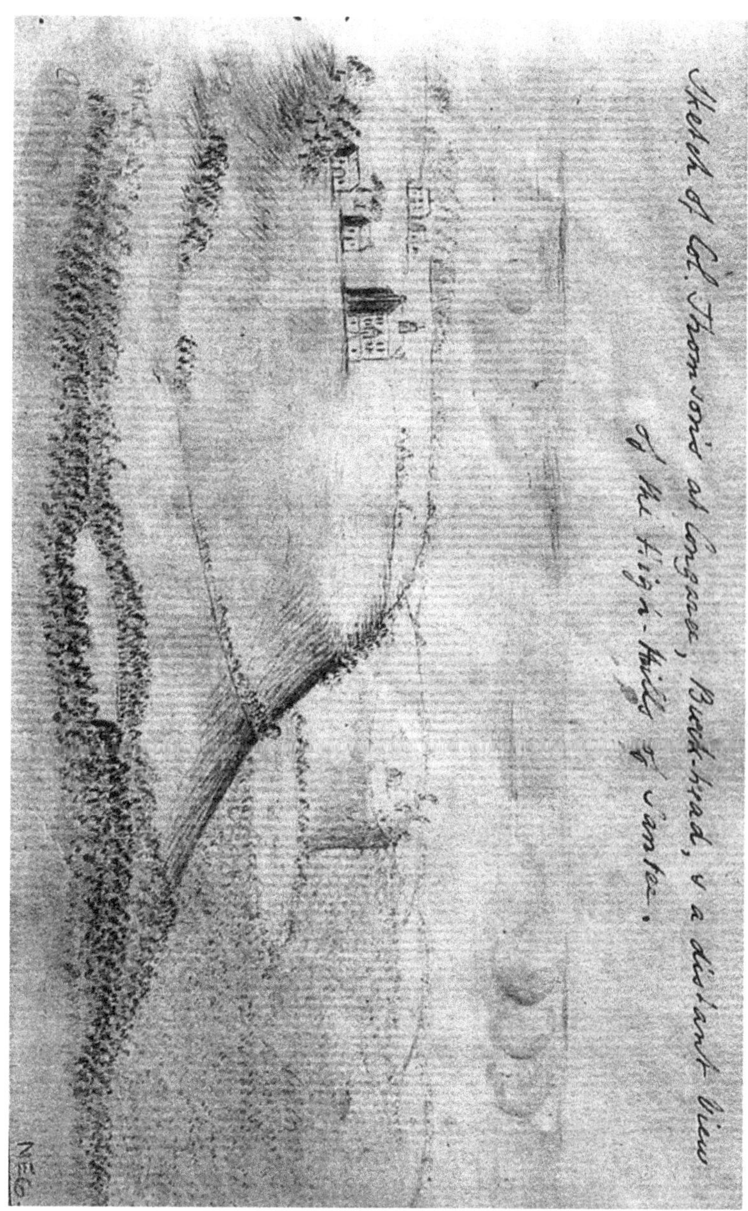

Figure 9. "Sketch of Col. Thomson at Congaree, Buck-head, & distant View of the High-Hills of Santee" possibly by William Drayton, ca. 1784. Note Thomson in foreground left, Motte behind Thomson, and the Old Farmhouse to the right. (*Courtesy of South Carolina Historical Society, Addlestone Library of the College of Charleston*)

(i.e., Thomson) were rebels and would lose their property and possibly their lives. There was yet another reason to occupy Belleville. The British had plans to persuade or pressure Thomson into joining the British cause. While at Belleville on June 7, Balfour wrote Lord Charles Cornwallis that Thomson "is the leading man here [Congarees to Nelson's Ferry], and I am informed, although active on the other side, yet has not been harsh or oppressive, and from a good many reasons I believe he may be made useful in taking the other side, especially as he is fond of money." Balfour continued that "if he cannot be brought to act for us, he ought to be sent away from this part of the country immediately."[6] Balfour repeats that sentiment on the ninth, stating again that Thomson should either take an active role as a Loyalist or be sent away.[7] Cornwallis, though, disapproved of converting former rebels, writing, "I cannot approve of admitting any officers of the Rebel militia into ours for the present."[8] Thus, Thomson senior was sent to Charleston.

Thomson was not the only prominent landowner in the area of interest to the British. While at Belleville, Balfour wrote that "Old Mr. Middleton and Mr. Motte" were people "of this place" who "mean to be with you [Cornwallis] soon." Old Middleton was Henry Middleton, a very wealthy and extensive landowner who was active in the rebellion and was elected to the Continental Congress in 1774 and continued to actively participate in the rebellion's political realm as a member of the Provincial Congress in South Carolina. Balfour described Jacob Motte as "a man of property to whom a confinement to his plantation *here* [italics in the original] might be of use." So, Jacob Motte was also being considered as a possible prominent personage that might be turned to the British. Eventually, Middleton did indeed abandon the revolution, swearing allegiance to the crown.[9]

Despite Balfour's statement that it was necessary to have a post at Belleville, it is not clear that the plantation was continuously occupied by the British through the summer and fall of 1780. For instance, Cornwallis wrote to Balfour on June 20 that he was going to meet with Major Graham on the way back to Charleston and send the detachments at the Congarees, and perhaps those at Belleville, to Camden and Charleston.[10] Then there is another odd letter from Lieutenant Colonel Alex Innes of the South Carolina Royalists on July 24 stating that he saw rebels at Thomson's and wanted to clean them out if he had the time.[11] These suggest that there was not a camp at Belleville that summer. Then in late August, Colonel John Fisher of the Royal Orangeburg militia recorded that a detachment of the regiment had arrived there on the twenty-fourth on their way down to Nelson's Ferry. Fisher was a prominent Orangeburg District resident whom the British made a colonel after deciding Thomson was not to be trusted. [12] Fisher reported that their service was not urgent, suggesting that the region was quiet.[13]

Indeed, through the early fall, Fisher, with his Orangeburg regiment, was keeping the Orangeburg region under control and British strategic concerns were focused on the region east of the Santee where Marion was commanding their attention with raids and ambushes. On October 26, Balfour, having returned from Ninety Six and appointed commandant in Charleston, reported to Rawdon the state of affairs in South Carolina, observing that a post was needed between Camden and Georgetown. Balfour lamented that generally, the Loyalist militia were not turning out, "the militia of Orangeburg and some of the Back Country excepted." Further, "The Orangeburg regiment, I think, should always be left to guard the Santee."[14]

Sometime that fall the British arrived for an extended occupation and fortified the Thomson house. Possibly it was before November 1780.[15] Whenever the forting-up began, the post at Belleville was formidable when completed. The house was surrounded by a palisade, with outbuildings incorporated into the defenses. Sometime after it was fortified, young William made a desperate but successful escape. He and a sentinel went running after a loose pig, and William kept running, eventually to join Sumter's brigade.[16] Meanwhile, Colonel Thomson became ill in Charleston and was permitted to return home where he would remain until he was exchanged later in the war.

It may not have been the best place to convalesce. Orangeburg County historian Salley recorded that the British ransacked the plantation, taking his horses, livestock, and his slaves, with as many as one hundred slaves lost to smallpox and camp fever.[17] By their own admission, the British regularly raided sequestered estates throughout the war until the plantations were stripped of everything useful, and the slaves, if not confiscated, were left destitute. If the British did not requisition food, forage, and slaves, roving bands of American militia would.[18]

The British were active at and around Belleville in November and December. The Orangeburg militia were ordered to secure nearby Manigault's Ferry on the first of November.[19] On the third, an aide wrote Lord Cornwallis that a Captain Coffin had taken ill at Colonel Thomson's enroute to Camden, and also reported that "parties of rebells lay lurking in that country, that twenty has been seen together."[20] In December, British reinforcements arrived in Charleston and were sent north to join Lord Cornwallis. On their march, they took the western route, called the "common road," despite the fact that Balfour had described it as being "stript of every thing."[21] They arrived at Thomson's on December 26.[22] Balfour may have made the trip with the reinforcements as Cornwallis wrote Rawdon that Balfour could not make it in a day to Cornwallis from Thomson's.[23] Upon their arrival, the new recruits were bound to be greatly disappointed as Rawdon informed Cornwallis that there was no rum at Thomson's on Christmas Day.[24]

Several letters that fall and winter between Balfour, Rawdon, and Cornwallis mention a supply depot at McCord's Ferry. It's very possible these letters actually refer to nearby Thomson's, or perhaps there was a post at McCord's also. For example, Balfour mentions keeping "four mounted infantry" at McCord's that December. That suggests that they were physically at McCord's Ferry. However, back in June, the Prince of Wales flank companies were reported to be at McCord's, which were obviously those same troops posted at Thomson's, thus suggesting McCord's and Thomson's might have been the same locality from the British perspective.[25] They were only a little more than a mile apart.

On January 29, 1781, Francis Marion sent Major James Postell and Captain John Postell across the Santee on raids against British posts. John Postell burned British supplies at Wadboo Bridge and Keithfield Plantation. James was supposed to burn the supplies at Thomson's but found no stores there, having "been carried away a few days before," so turning to nearby Manigault's Ferry only two miles away, he found stores of sugar, flour, pork, and clothing in a British redoubt, with only four men in it. He destroyed the supplies and took the soldiers prisoner.[26] The lack of supplies at Thomson's is curious. Certainly, the plantation was still occupied by the British, as will be seen. Given what would happen the following month, it's possible James decided the fort was too strong, and there were no supplies outside the fort worth the risk.

On February 21 or 22, 1781, Thomas Sumter surrounded the fort at Belleville. Previously, he had laid siege to Fort Granby, located along the Congaree River (in modern West Columbia, South Carolina). That siege failed when British reinforcements from Camden appeared on the opposite riverbank, forcing Sumter to break off the attack. The British expected Sumter to retreat north to safety; instead, he proceeded downstream to Belleville.

When Sumter arrived before Belleville, it was occupied by only some light infantry under the command of Captain Morris Robinson.[27] Sumter, lacking artillery but with perhaps as many as seven hundred militia, surrounded the post and throughout the day exchanged fire with the defenders.[28] Losing patience, in the late afternoon, Sumter foolishly decided to attack the fortified plantation in a rush across an open field. Although Sumter's men managed to get to the fort and set fire to some of the outbuildings, they were forced back, and the fires were put out. William Thomson was in the house at the time, perhaps wondering what was going to happen to his mansion.[29]

Sumter withdrew from Belleville, leaving a few men behind to continue harassing the fort while he and the rest of his force camped either at Manigault's plantation or ferry.[30] There he learned of a supply convoy from Charleston moving up the Charleston road that passed between Thomson's and Buckhead. About a mile south of Manigault's Ferry he attacked the convoy, killing thirteen soldiers, capturing sixty-six, and most importantly, obtaining twenty supply wagons.[31] Besides much needed supplies, two trunks of gold and silver coins were captured.[32] Then, shortly after the capture, Sumter was forced to raise his siege of Belleville when he learned of the approach of another British relief force under Lord Rawdon. Again, he turned south, putting the captured supplies on barges and floating them downstream toward Fort Watson, his next planned target. Unfortunately, the man Sumter hired to guide the barges downstream, Robert Livingston, was either incompetent or a Loyalist.[33] Approaching Fort Watson, the guide promptly steered the barges to the British where they overcame Sumter's guards and reclaimed their supplies. A frustrated Sumter made a brief attack on a British foraging party near the fort on February 28 and then withdrew north.[34] Those same supplies would eventually be recaptured by Marion and Lee in April.

THE BRITISH OCCUPY FORT MOTTE

Sometime in the late winter or early spring of 1781, the British began fortifying Rebecca Motte's new Mount Joseph Plantation mansion. When and why remains a mystery. As noted, the primary documents do little to elucidate what was happening at Mount Joseph during the period between January and May 1781.

As to when, it might have been as early as December, but more likely it began in January, when the British went on a construction spree, to include an abatis around the Camden fortifications and the construction of what became Fort Granby under the command of Major Andrew Maxwell.[35] Nisbet Balfour wrote Lieutenant Charles McPherson on January 21, 1781, requesting that Lieutenant McPherson "keep an eye on the Passages between you & Nelson's Ferry."[36] There is no direct evidence where McPherson was at that time; however, when Fort Motte was completed, he became its commandant. He may very well have been at Belleville as historian Robert Bass asserts. Thus, there is some possibility that while Sumter attacked Belleville, only a mile away the British were in the process of supervising slaves constructing Fort Motte around Rebecca Motte's house. Possibly Sumter's raid delayed the construction of Fort Motte.

Henry Lee, admittedly not the most reliable eyewitness, stated that Mrs. Motte's home was "a large, new mansion-house."[37] Exactly what he meant by "new" is subject to debate; however, it seems that it must have been very new when the fort was built around it. Archaeological excavations at the house support this conjecture. The kitchen artifact assemblage in the immediate area of the mansion consisted of 1,179 sherds of which only 394, or 33 percent, dated to the eighteenth century, the rest being part of the nineteenth-century occupation. Of the eighteenth-century artifacts, 191 (or 48 percent of the eighteenth-century assemblage) were creamware sherds. Creamware was a late eighteenth-century ceramic, common on sites of the revolutionary period and popular until the early nineteenth century (generally 1762 to 1820). Thus, the ceramic assemblage suggests that the eighteenth-century occupation of the site began in the late eighteenth century.[38] There is no archaeological evidence of an earlier occupation of Mount Joseph hill.

Whenever Mrs. Motte began building her house it must be considered that during this time of warfare, gathering building materials, including wood timbers, iron fittings, and constructing a house would have been quite a feat.[39] As will be described in the next chapter, it was a formidable, possibly three-story edifice. Certainly, slave labor was involved, supervised by Jacob and Rebecca.

As to why, historian Hugh F. Rankin suggests the outpost "had been moved to take advantage of the better terrain at Mount Pleasant [*sic*] Plantation."[40] This probably can be dismissed. Belleville was closer to the main road to McCord's Ferry than Mount Joseph and was a better location for troops to monitor road traffic both there and on the road north to Ninety Six. Neither location, however, was ideal for guarding McCord's Ferry, which was over a mile from both. And we know the British had guards and perhaps a depot at the ferry. Perhaps they had a redoubt there also, as they did at Nelson's Ferry and Manigault's Ferry. In 1813, Francis Rawdon responded by letter to Henry Lee concerning Lee's portrayal of Rawdon's role in the hanging of an American named Isaac Hayne. Rawdon defended himself as not being involved, as he was in charge of the upcountry. As part of his defense, Rawdon noted that the region of the Santee, Congaree, and Saluda Rivers was under the jurisdiction of Nisbet Balfour, not himself. Further, he claimed Lord Cornwallis "debarred" him from interfering with Balfour's authority in that region. Rawdon even claimed that his post at Camden, with few resources in the region, defended nothing and left him vulnerable to being cut off (as he ultimately was):

> I was completely dependent on Lieutenant-Colonel Balfour for subsistence, for military stores, for horses, for arms, and for those re-enforcements which were indispensable from the expenditure of men, in the unceasing activity of our service. With his posts at Motte's house, Congaree, and Ninety-Six, I had no concern, further than their occasional danger obliged me to make movements for their protection; an assistance which I had particular difficulty in rendering to the two former, from the works having unaccountably been so placed as to not command the ferries, through which blunder succors could not be thrown across the river to the garrisons when invested by an enemy.[41]

So, abandoning and destroying the fortified post at Belleville and then making considerable effort to fortify Mrs. Motte's new home was not done for tactical purposes. Perhaps it was simply part of an overall construction improvement effort by the British.

Overall, the most reasonable explanation, although far from conclusive, is that the British did not occupy Mrs. Motte's plantation home in June of 1780 or through the fall, because there was no house to fortify until late winter/early spring 1781. Once finished, a couple months later, the British abandoned Belleville and began to construct a fort around Rebecca's newly finished house.

On April 7, Thomas Sumter reported to Greene that "the Post at Co' Thompson's is Broke up & the Troops removed to the Congarees, Where there is five Two pound pieces [*sic*] of artillery, & one wall piece."[42] Sumter may have assumed the troops went to Fort Granby at the Congarees. But it is also very possible they simply moved the short distance to the new fort at Motte's. Further, the supply convoy that Sumter attacked possibly was bringing supplies to the new post.[43]

Fort Motte certainly seems to have just sprung up through thin air overnight. In February 1781, Belleville was the principal depot along the western road to Camden and Ninety Six. Then in April, it's "broken up." It's not until late April that the British, for the first time, mention a post at Mount Joseph. On April 20, 1781, Colonel Nisbet Balfour reported to Lord Cornwallis on the various posts and their detachments in South Carolina. Balfour reported that "at Motte's House, [there were] 54 infantry."[44]

The first time the Americans mention a fort at Motte's is Thomas Sumter's letter to General Greene on May 2. In it, Sumter reports on the distribution of British detachments in the central region of South Carolina, stating, "The Hessian horse is Gone Downwards Except Twenty five that Crossed from the fort at Motts & Went in to Camden With Maj Doyl." Sumter also notes that the British "Maj Maxwell Keeps pretty Close.[45] Those at Mr. Motts Very much so. They are digging for water. Will obtain it with Very Great Difficulty, but may be Cut of [*sic*] from it, with a pice of artillery as it is out Side the fort. I think this place May be Taken with a Sixpounder."[46] Three days later, Marion and Lee arrive to make the attempt.[47]

FIVE

The Siege and Capture of Fort Motte

AROUND TEN O'CLOCK ON THE COLD, rainy morning of Sunday, May 6, 1781, General Francis Marion and Colonel Henry Lee arrived before Fort Motte.[1] With Marion, there were only around 150 men.[2] Lee's legion consisted maybe of 100 dragoons and 148 infantry.[3] But the Americans also had the 6-pounder cannon under the command of Captain Finley and the escort of North Carolina Continentals under Major Pinketham Eaton, formerly militiamen who had fled at the battle of Guilford Court House and were sentenced into Continental service for one year as punishment.[4] Still, it was not a large army for a siege.

Opposing the Americans was a detachment of 184 British regulars, Hessians, and Provincials.[5] The British consisted of eighty officers and men of the 2nd Battalion, 84th Regiment of Foot (sixty-nine enlisted), under the command of Captain Neil Campbell.[6] The newly raised and green-jacketed Hessians included fifty-nine officers and men (fifty-one enlisted) of Frederich Starcloff's troop of Light Dragoons under the command of Corporal John Ludvick.[7] There were also some forty-five Provincials under the command of Loyalist Levi Smith, who had not officially been commissioned as their leader. Included in the total mix of defenders were an unknown number of dragoons who had been escorting supplies and had arrived the day before Marion and Lee.[8] They arrived not only with supplies but also a carronade.[9] The post commander was Captain-Lieutenant Charles McPherson.[10] There was one other Lieutenant, either Lieutenant Robert Amiel of the 17th Foot or Second Lieutenant Walter Partridge of the 23rd Foot.[11] Overall, it was quite a large command for the new fort.

Marion and Lee could not have felt overly confident of their chances against such a force and formidable edifice. Marion wrote to General Greene that the post was "Obstinate, and strong," which could describe both the British detachment and the fort.[12] On a commanding 245-foot bluff, Mrs. Motte had built her mansion.[13] An engineer's drawing of the fort, depicting it in plan and profile, shows the three-story, hipped roof, the house closely enclosed by an imposing wood and earthen fortification beginning only a few feet from the house (Figure 10).[14] The wall consisted of an interior three-step banquette to a log palisade that rose some nine feet from the ground, protecting the first floor and most of the second. Thrown against the outside of the palisade was an earthen glacis ten to eleven feet wide. The dirt for this glacis came from about a seven-foot wide, six-foot deep ditch, squared off at the base of the ditch to form a flat three-foot floor. Beyond the ditch, some twenty to thirty feet away, was a row of abatis trees placed with their branches outward, an effective barrier to any rush of infantry against the fort. On two opposite northwest and southeast corners were log blockhouses with firing slits. Altogether, the fort was depicted as a rectangle 115 by 125 feet exterior, ditch-edge to ditch-edge.[15]

That was how an American engineer depicted it. Ground-penetrating radar of the fort clearly indicates a rectangular fort with

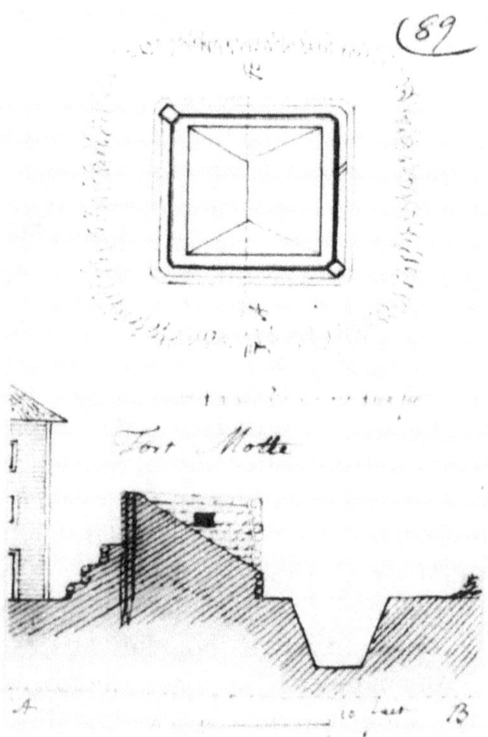

Figure 10. Engineer's Drawing of Fort Motte. (*Papers of the Continental Engineers*)

rounded corners, the long axis northwest to southeast, and the distance from exterior ditch-edge to ditch-edge being 131 feet northwest to southeast by 115 feet northeast to southwest. Inside the ditch the fort was probably 120 by 100 feet (Figure 11).[16] An archaeological cross-section of the ditch shows some minor deviation, the ditch appearing to be about 9 feet wide and the floor being V-shaped instead of flat (Figure 12).[17] The back of the house probably faced the river to the north and west, while a small plaza, or front yard, was formed by the palisade to the southeast. Excavations inside the fort revealed two chimney bases about 44 feet apart. This would be typical of a traditional I-house, with two 16-foot rooms and a 12-foot enclosed dogtrot between, how-

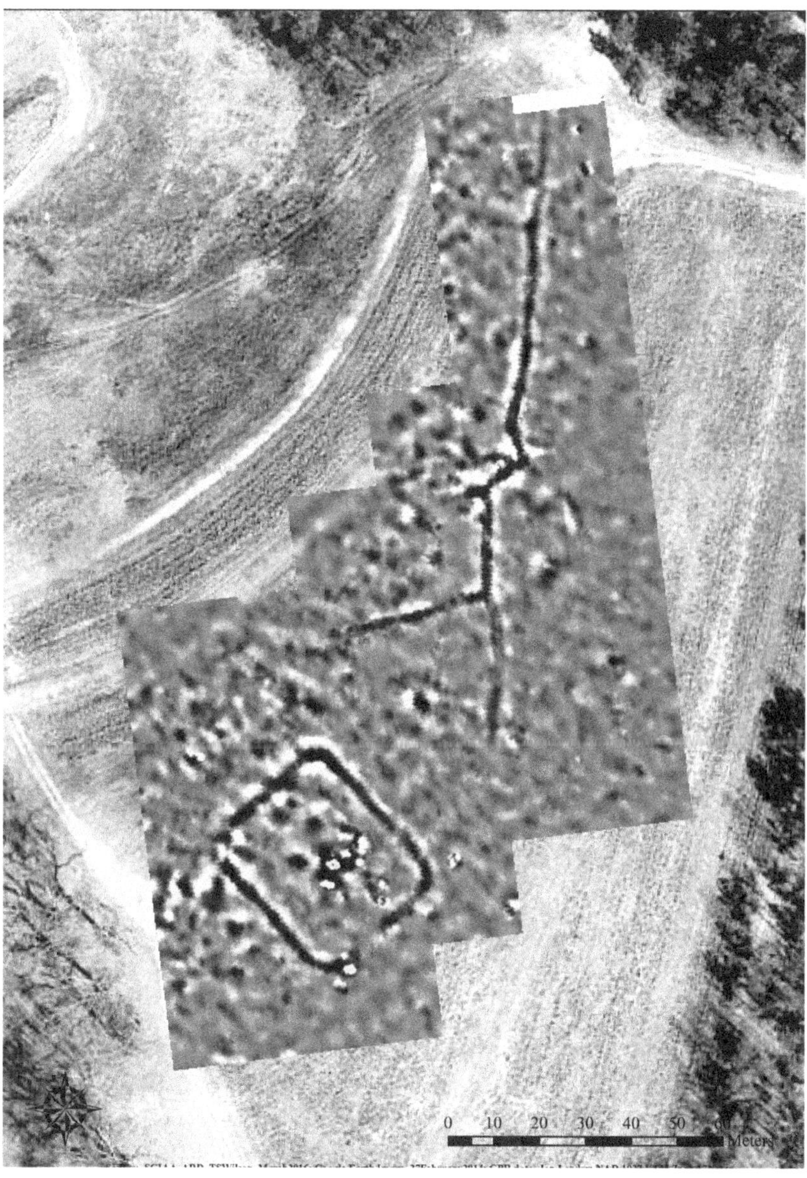

Figure 11. Ground Penetrating Radar of Fort Motte and American Sap. Note the western parallel continued west another twenty feet. (*John Leader, courtesy SCIAA*)

ever, it is not clear that they are Motte's chimneys or from a later nineteenth-century house built after the Motte mansion burned down. Also, I-houses do not typically have hipped roofs so there is the possibility that the house was square as depicted in the engineer's drawing. Traditionally, the house would have faced a road coming to the house and this is supported by a gate in the southeast corner of the fort. Into this plaza, the 184 British, Hessians, and Loyalists quickly crammed themselves and there they would remain throughout the siege.[18]

Just outside the fort's northeastern ditch was the well (mentioned in chapter 4), which Sumter reported the British were digging on May 2, another suggestion that Fort Motte was only finished in April and was quite new when Marion arrived, and that the Mottes had not had time to dig a well.[19] It's possible this well was connected to the fort with a covered way, as had been done at Fort Watson.[20]

Upon arrival, Lee's cavalry quickly captured Loyalist Levi Smith as he was walking downhill from the fort to his house for breakfast, and perhaps there was a brief exchange of gunfire as the British rushed into the fort.[21] Then Marion deployed his militia around the house.

The recovery of lead shot from the area around the fort provides clues as to the distribution of Marion's troops (Figures 13 and 14). It appears from the distribution of fired and unfired buckshot that Marion deployed most of his small army along a tree line across an open field, a little over one hundred yards to the south and east of the fort (Figure 14).[22] Because there is a gradual downward slope from the house westward and then a sharp drop around one hundred yards away, there would have been little use in placing many men there, except a guard as a precaution against escape. Thus, with riflemen to the east and south, a few men below the fort cliffside to the west, and with a long open field extending to the woods some two hundred yards to the north, the British were effectively surrounded. Marion established a camp in a "declivity" downhill from Mount Joseph five hundred yards east of the fort, safe from British fire (Figure 13).

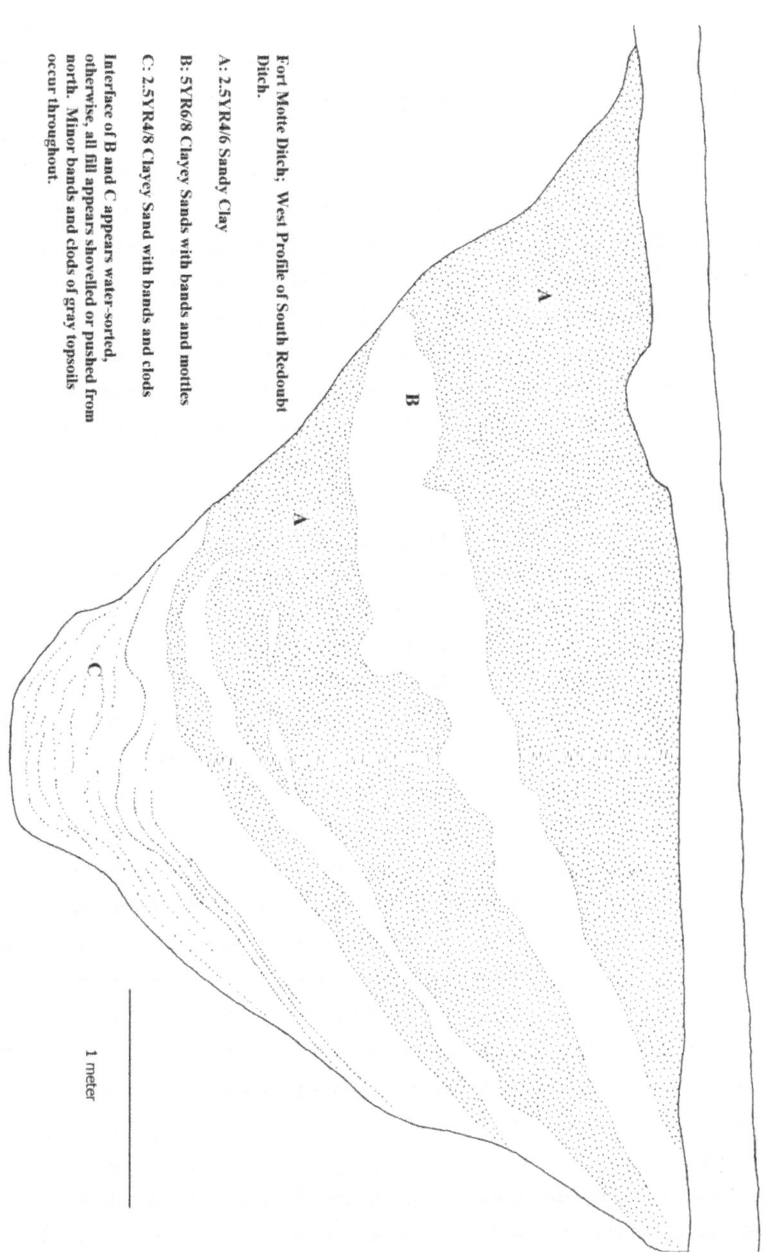

Figure 12. Cross-section of Fort Motte Ditch. Note bottom and middle layer soil appear water sorted indicating exposure to rain and therefore two separate filling episodes. (*James Legg, courtesy SCIAA*)

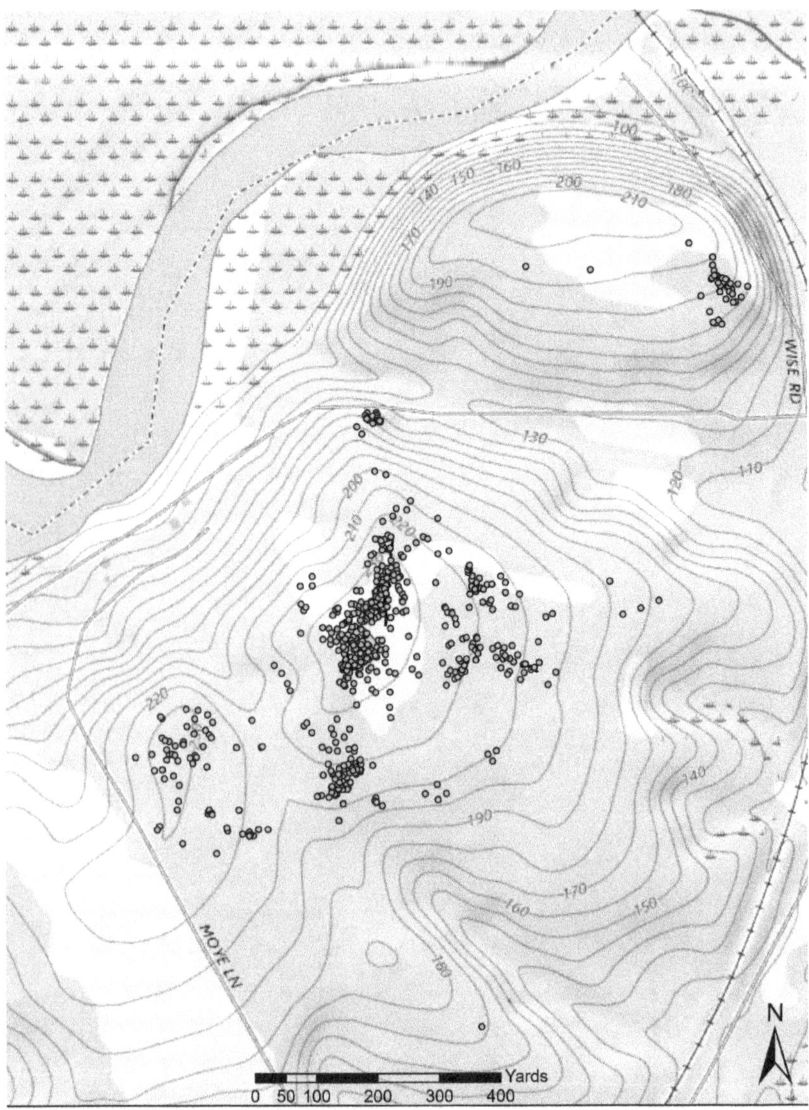

Figure 13. Topographic Map of Fort Motte and General Distribution of Lead Shot. Center artifact cluster: around house and American sap; two clusters to left: Marion's men and artillery mound; two clusters below: camps of unidentified soldiers, possibly Greene's post-siege Continental Army camps. (*John Fisher, courtesy SCIAA*)

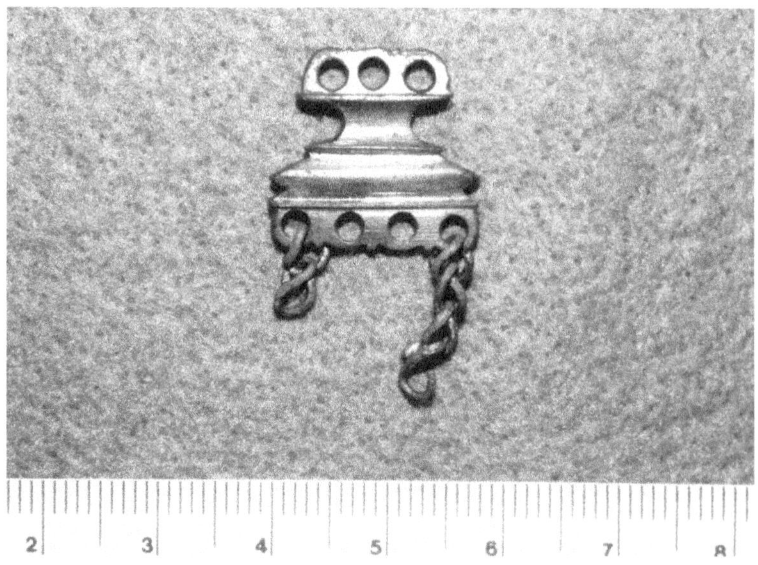

Figure 14. Fragment of a Chatelaine, possibly owned by Mrs. Rebecca Motte. It was recovered at the base of the hill where the "Old Farmhouse" and Lee's Continentals camped. (*James Legg, courtesy SCIAA*)

He had so few men, that it could not have been a very large camp.[23] Marion made his headquarters at Thomson's, where he no doubt discussed strategy with William Thomson.[24] Meanwhile, Lee and the Legion established their main camp across the divide on Buckhead Hill, where the overseer's or "old farmhouse" stood, the house the Mottes first occupied when they arrived the previous June (Figure 13).

Sometime shortly before or right after the arrival of Marion and Lee, McPherson ordered the Motte contingent out of the fort and exiled back across the vale to their old "overseer's" house.[25] When Lee arrived, Mrs. Motte was there and invited Lee to stay at the house (Figure 14):

and not only the lieutenant-colonel, but every officer of his corps, off duty, daily experienced her liberal hospitality, politely proffered, and as politely administered. . . . While her richly-spread table presented with taste and fashion all the luxuries of her opulent country, and her sideboard offered without reserve the best wines of Europe—antiquated relic of happier days—her active benevolence found its way to the sick and wounded; cherishing with softest kindness infirmity and misfortune, converting despair into hope, and nursing debility into strength.[26]

Neither Marion nor Lee was going to order their men to storm this well-protected fort as Sumter had tried at Belleville in February. After charging across an open field, they would have had to face the tree abatis and such a delay would have been suicidal. The clear fields of fire surrounding the house probably precluded the idea of employing a wooden tower like they had used against Fort Watson. Instead, a plan was formed to dig a sap or trench to the fort's abatis. Once the sap was dug to a location just outside the abatis, the Continentals could charge the fort with fixed bayonets while their 6-pounder raked the fort with iron canister to keep the British from defending the walls. To do this, they would need laborers to dig the sap and a mound on which to place the 6-pounder, thereby elevating the cannon to the level of the top of the palisade.

Thus, Marion's first task was to gather slaves from Mrs. Motte, Colonel Thomson, and other neighbors including those of William Bull.[27] This was easily accomplished and work soon began. Lee states he established a camp "400 yards" directly north of the fort where the deep vale between the two hills dropped off. This is an overestimate. The beginning of the sap was closer, about two hundred yards from the fort as indicated in the ground-penetrating radar image (Figures 11 and 15).[28] "Relays of working parties being provided for every four hours, and some of the negroes from the neighboring plantations being brought, by the influence of Marion, to our assistance, the works advanced with rapidity."[29] East of the fort, 250 yards and slightly downhill, more laborers began the construction of the artillery mound, which consisted of digging out dirt and piling it in front of the hole (Figure 16). Eventually, the mound would be around ten feet high.[30]

For the next four days Lee's Continentals and slaves dug the sap toward the house, while Marion's riflemen fired at the fort.

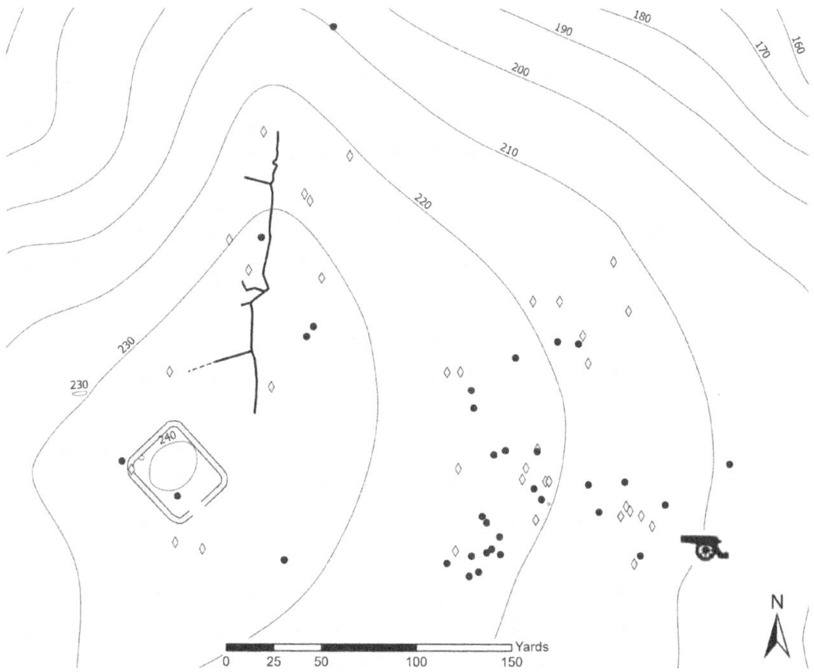

Figure 15. Distribution of Fired and Unfired Buckshot Near Fort Motte. Diamond: fired buckshot; Dot: unfired buckshot. Note cannon icon indicating location of artillery mound. (*John Fisher, courtesy SCIAAA*)

The hilltop north of the fort was open and level; however, about 120 yards from the fort there began a gradual descent continuing northward to the sap entrance. This allowed the sappers some protection to dig straight south toward the fort for the first seventy-five yards. The Americans excavated a short parallel to the sap possibly for soldiers or slaves to step aside for someone to pass. Once the sap reached the level crest, however, the sappers had to zigzag the trench toward the fort in the classic style of eighteenth-century siege warfare, and they most assuredly pushed a barrel in front of their sap so that they could advance the trench by digging below it and pushing it forward. Just after the crest, the soldiers and slaves also dug a longer parallel to return the British fire, who were desperately attempting to kill the excavators or at least delay their progress (Figures 11 and 15).

Figure 16. Artillery Mound in the 1840s. (*Benson Lossing, 1850*)

Fired musket balls archaeologically recovered along the sap indicate that the British were taking deliberate aim at the soldier or slave in front doing the digging behind the barrel (Figure 17). Normally, a smooth-bore musket would not have been accurate enough to guarantee a hit on an individual target ninety yards away. The fired .75-caliber musket balls recovered along the sap, however, were banded, suggesting that either the British were ramming their .75-caliber musket balls into a smaller bore musket, probably a French .69-caliber Charleville musket, or were increasing the normal black powder charge, either of which would slightly increase accuracy.[31] The British also fired iron canister at the diggers using the carronade that had arrived the day before the siege began (Figure 18).[32]

As the sap excavations progressed, Marion's riflemen along the tree line to the east of the fort kept the British heads down behind their walls, keeping them from being able to volley fire along the sap. The distribution of American fired rifle balls indicates that most of the firing was coming from the south and southeast, with a dense cluster just to the west and outside the southeast gate (Figure 19).[33] Many of these probably had bounced off the palisade wall, hard clay glacis, or corner bastion. There are also fired

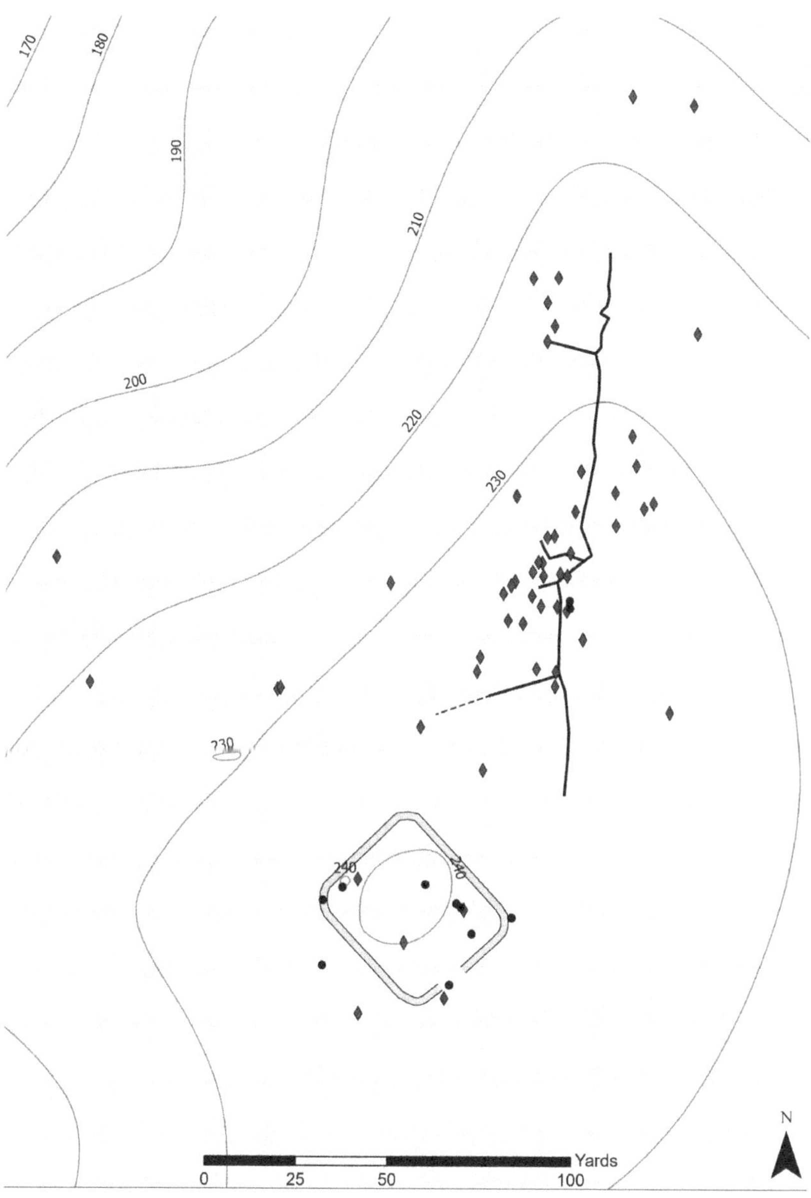

Figure 17. Distribution of Fired and Unfired .75-Caliber Lead Shot Along the Sap Line. Diamond: fired; Dot: unfired. (*John Fisher, courtesy SCIAA*)

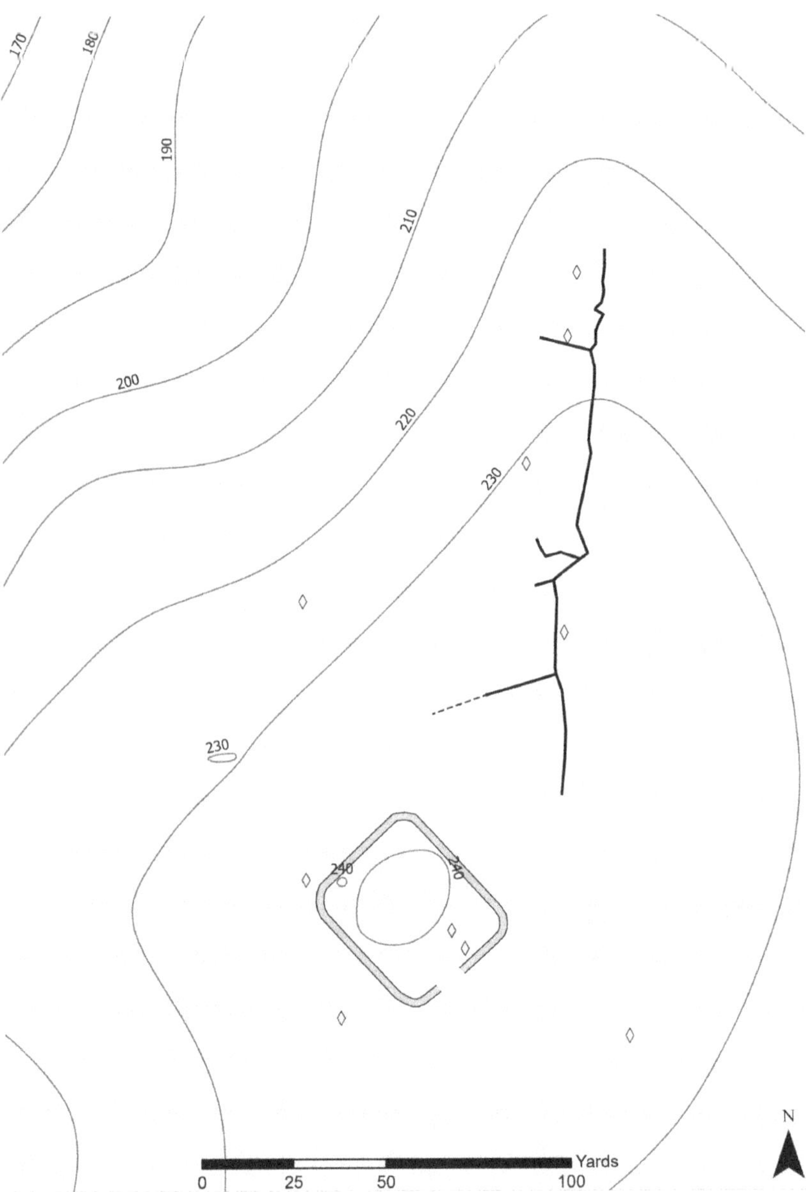

Figure 18. Canister at Fort Motte. Note American canister around fort and British canister along sap. (*John Fisher, Courtesy SCIAA*)

Figure 19. Distribution of Fired and Unfired Rifle Balls at Fort Motte. Diamond: fired; Dot: unfired. (*John Fisher, courtesy SCIAA*)

rifle balls west of the fort, although fewer, probably ricochet or overshots. The British, too, must have had a few rifles as there were fired rifle balls recovered along the sap and unfired balls inside the fort.

Around May 8 or 9, as the siege continued, Marion and Lee had a visit from General Thomas Sumter. Sumter had returned to the low country and as the siege of Fort Motte began, he was again laying siege at Fort Granby on the Congaree River. On May 6, he wrote Greene that he thought he would not be able to take Granby, but that Motte could be taken in three or four days.[34] Sometime after May 7, he left behind a detachment to continue a blockade and marched with the rest of his troops for the British post at Orangeburg, stopping by Fort Motte. Sumter left a few more troops with Lee and continued south, arriving in front of Orangeburg post on May 10. The next day some ninety men and officers surrendered, and Sumter gained plentiful provisions and supplies.[35]

MARION'S PIQUE

An argument can be made that the American success in the Southern Campaign of the American Revolution owes much to the leadership of General Nathanael Greene. Part of that leadership was his ability to work with and around several sensitive egos. Sumter was one, Lee was one, and Marion was surely another.

A major source of frustration for Marion revolved around his militia. Throughout the fall of 1780 and into the spring of 1781, Marion's plans were often thwarted by the vacillating nature of their commitment. There was a core of soldiers who kept to the field despite the circumstances, but many, perhaps most, of his men came and went in a constant stream. For instance, pension applications note veterans stating that they joined Marion or Sumter, then joined the other in midsiege at Fort Motte. Thomas Young, for instance, volunteered with Captain Joseph Hugs and "marched to Buck Head & attended the siege of that fort. But before that fort was taken, went off with a detachment against Orangeburg & took that fort under the command of Genl.

Sumter."[36] It didn't seem to matter if Marion had just been chased across the low country, or had just won a battle, they showed up for a while and then left at inopportune times. Marion had to adjust his plans accordingly. As noted, Marion only took eighty men to Fort Watson, and some left due to smallpox during the siege. He had to detach some troops under Major John Ervin to the Pee Dee to avenge the death of Colonel Kolb; that detachment was still searching for the culprits.[37] He was lucky to be able to report he had 150 men when he arrived at Fort Motte, which was a fairly large number in comparison to his usual command the previous fall.

Meanwhile, Greene had been pressing Marion for horses since January, which compounded Marion's personnel problem. Greene had long wanted to raise a larger cavalry unit, recognizing the importance of a mounted troop to gather intelligence, to screen his army, to prevent being surprised by the enemy, and to ambush the enemy in a surprise attack. Greene wrote Thomas Jefferson that "Superior Cavalry is of the greatest importance to the salvation of this country and without them you would soon hear of detachments being cut to p[i]eces in every quarter."[38] A cavalry unit obviously needs horses, and horses were in short supply for both sides of the conflict. That January Greene asked Marion to round up horses in the Pee Dee region around Marion's camp at Snow's Island. Marion replied at that time that he had only "twenty small horse very poor & ordinary," which was quite possibly a lie.[39] Or perhaps Marion was quibbling, answering that he only had that many horses that were not the personal property of his militia. Greene kept pressing. He again reminded Marion to gather horses when he ordered him across the Santee at the end of April.[40] Unknown to Marion, Greene had been prompted by Lee and Sumter, both of whom wrote Greene that Marion could supply Greene; Lee noting that Marion could supply "150 dragoon horses," and Sumter adding "Gen Marion is also in the Way of Getting Good Horses."[41]

It is not clear whether Greene understood that the only horses Marion had were those owned by his men, but he should have.

In any case, Marion's frustrations with fickle militia and horses finally boiled over. On the opening day of the siege, upon another request for horses, Marion angrily replied:

> I acknowledge that you have repeatedly mention the want of Dragoon horses & wish it had been in my power to furnh them but it is not nor never had been. The few horses which has been taken from [Torrey's?] has been kept for the service & never for private property, but if you think it best for the service to Dismount the Malitia now with me I will Direct Col Lee & Cap Conyers to do so, but am sertain we shall never git their service in future. This would not give me any uneasiness as I have somtime Determin to relinquish my command in the malitia as soon as you arrived in it & I wish to do it as soon as this post is Either taken or abandoned.
>
> I Shall assist in reducing the post here & when Col. Lee returns to you I Take that oppertunity in waiting on you when I hope to get permission to go to Philadelphia.[42]

Marion was most assuredly correct that taking the militia's horses would cause resentment that would further deplete his ranks. Fortunately, Greene wisely got the point and backed off. He responded with a masterful letter to assuage Marion's ego. He wrote first with words of friendship: "I shall be always happy to see you at head Quarters; but cannot think you can seriously mean to solicit leave to go to Philadelphia." Then an appreciation of what Marion had done to this point, followed by an appeal to Marion's sense of duty: "It is true your task has been disagreeable; but not more so than others. . . . Your State has been invaded, your all is at stake. What has been done will signify nothing unless we persevere to the end." Next, Greene backs off his request for horses, recognizing the need for a mounted militia: "It is not my wish to take the horses from the Militia if it will injure the public service, the effects and consequences you can better judge of than I can." Finally, he ends with a compliment: "You have rendered important services to the public with the Militia under your command; and done great honor to yourself and I would not wish to render your situation less agreeable with them unless it is to answer some very great purpose and this I perswade my self you would agree to from a desire to promote the common good."[43]

There is an absence of correspondence between Marion and Greene between May 6 and 11, which may mean that Marion continued to slowly simmer, or both were just too busy. While the soldiers and slaves dug toward the fort, Marion had little to do, but his scouts continued to bring him intelligence. On May 10, Marion wrote two letters to Sumter, the first warning him of a small party of the enemy riding toward him, and later that day, that Rawdon had abandoned Camden.[44] Finally, responding to Greene on May 11, Marion revealed what had been frustrating him for months:

> I assure you I am very serious in my intention of relinquishing my Malitia Command; not that I wish to Shrink from fatigue or trouble, or for any private Interest but because I found Little is to be done with such men as I have, who Leave me very Often at the very point of Executing a plan & their Late infamous behavior in Quiting me at a time which required their service must confirm me in my former Intentions. If I cannot act in the malitia I cannot see any service I can be, to remain in the state & I hope by going to the Northward to fall in some employ where I may have an Opertunity of serving the United States, in some way that I cannot be in this Country.[45]

Nevertheless, he saw the necessity of backing off a bit also, closing the May 11 letter with a note saying that he had sent Greene a horse for his personal use and would try to get more.

Marion's foul mood also affected his relationship with Colonel Lee. Lee, of course, had worked with Marion in late January when they had attempted a coordinated attack against Georgetown. Although the attack failed, Marion and Lee developed a friendship. Marion had written that "Colonel Lee's Interprising Genuis promises much."[46] Lee had noticed a moody Marion back while they were laying siege to Fort Watson, requesting Greene to write to Marion who was feeling "neglected." Yet at that time he was quite happy working with Marion, following up three days later writing Greene again that he would like to remain under Marion's command, which would please Marion, who he admires.[47] Standing before Fort Motte, however, Lee now writes Greene that he finds himself "deceived in [Marion]. He is inadequate & very discontented—this discontent arises from his nature."[48] Greene, demonstrating his mastery of human nature, assuages Lee's concerns about Marion and Sumter, writing the next day to "be careful, be cautious, be prudent, and above all attentive; This, with men as well as with ladies, goes a great way."[49]

Later, with the war in the distant past, Lee looked back at Marion with fondness. Lee remembered in his postwar memoirs that Marion "was virtuous all over; never even in manner, much less in reality, did he trench upon right. Beloved by his friends, and respected by his enemies, he exhibited a luminous example of the beneficial effects to be produced by an individual, who, with only means at his command, possesses a virtuous heart, a strong head, and a mind devoted to common good."[50] At the moment though, Marion and Lee were getting on each other's nerves.

Clearly, during the siege of Forts Watson and Motte, Francis Marion, the Swamp Fox, the consummate partisan warrior, was stewing with frustration about the capriciousness of his militia and contemplating giving up and going north (probably to Congress or Washington) to offer his services. He was not alone! At the same time he was bolstering Marion, Nathanael Greene was also suffering from a loss of confidence. William R. Davie remembered a conversation he had with Greene around this time.[51] Greene contemplated resigning his command and going north to Virginia.[52] Greene, however, was focused on his own weaknesses, and had forgotten about Rawdon's. On May 9, Greene and Marion were pondering their failures and considering giving up. On May 10, their world changed.

RAWDON ABANDONS CAMDEN

Early on the morning of May 10, Lord Francis Rawdon and his detachment of British soldiers abandoned Camden. Back on May 6, General Greene had retreated to Rugeley's plantation, where Gates had camped before the disastrous battle of Camden in August 1780; then he crossed the Wateree River, west of Camden. Rawdon, meanwhile, was contemplating his own situation. While he appeared strong to Greene, Rawdon in fact, was quite weak. Many of his troops were ill or wounded. At the strategic level, he realized he would have to withdraw all British from the backcountry, including Ninety Six and Camden, and regroup along the Santee where he could get support from Charleston. The recent arrival of Lieutenant Colonel Watson provided some hope, but Watson informed him of the loss of Fort Watson and that Marion and Lee were besieging Fort Motte. Now Rawdon was caught between Greene and the American partisans and his supply line to Charleston about to be cut.

Rawdon decided to make a last desperate attempt to push Greene away, and on May 7, crossed the Wateree. There he found Greene had dug in behind Sawney's Creek and was too strongly placed to attack. Returning to Camden, he began the process of abandoning the town, destroying fortifications, dumping ammunition into the nearby creek, and sending the baggage wagons southward on the ninth. The next day, at 10:00 a.m. he marched out of Camden, heading south toward Nelson's Ferry along the eastern route to Camden. He left behind thirty men too sick to travel and an equal number of American prisoners as an exchange. Following behind his army were some Loyalist militia and "well affected neighbors along our route, together with the wives, children, Negroes and baggage of almost all of them."[53] From this point on, it would be the Americans who were on the strategic offensive in the Southern Campaign.

THE FALL OF FORT MOTTE

Meanwhile, as the British left Camden on the tenth, Lee's sap reached close enough to the fort's abatis that he decided it was time to offer McPherson another chance to surrender (Figures 20 and 21).[54] A messenger under a flag was sent to the fort with the request. McPherson declined. Sometime that same day, Marion received intelligence that Lord Rawdon might have abandoned Camden. At first, he thought it was just a large foraging party.[55] However, Rawdon's withdrawal was confirmed and somehow the British in the fort also learned the news. The following night, Rawdon's campfires were seen in the distance and both the besieged and besiegers believed that Rawdon was coming to the fort's relief.[56] While hope was revived inside the fort, Marion and Lee realized they had to act quickly before Rawdon could come to the rescue.

With the sap up to the abatis, and the British crammed tightly inside the fort, it was determined that if they could set fire to the house, the British must surrender or be burned alive.

Now it was time to turn to the Continentals with bayonets. Two straight parallels had been dug, one running off to the southwest facing the western wall of the fort and the rear of the house, the other running southeast and facing the northern fort wall and gable end of the house (Figures 14, 17, 18, 21). Lee's infantry manned the trenches, while the artillerymen prepared to fire canister at the house roof when it was burning, to keep the British from dousing the flames. Additional troops were placed around the battery in case the British decided to make a sally from the fort's gate. They were offered one last chance.

Dr. Irvine, of the Legion cavalry, was charged with the flag, and was instructed to communicate faithfully the inevitable destruction impending, and the impracticality of relief, as Lord Rawdon had not yet passed the Santee. He was to give assurance that longer perseverance in vain resistance would place the garrison at the mercy of the conqueror, who was not regardless of the policy of preventing waste of time by inflicting exemplary punishment, where resistance was maintained only to produce such waste.[57]

McPherson, like his brother officer McKay at Fort Watson, politely declined the invitation. It was noon, May 12, 1781, and the sun was bright, heating up the dry roof shakes topping the Mount Joseph mansion, making them extremely flammable.

One of the most popular legends of South Carolina's Revolutionary War past is the story of how the Americans set fire to the Motte roof. Henry Lee's memoirs provide the basic outline to the story that has been enhanced in legend and art ever since.

Figure 20. Excavated Portion of the Sap's Western Parallel. (*Author, courtesy SCIAA*)

Mrs. Motte and her family were at the old farmhouse at the top of Buckhead Hill. As mentioned, Lee's men camped around the house and Rebecca insisted that Lee make his headquarters at her farmhouse. As the siege progressed, he and all his officers had enjoyed her hospitality, food, and of course, her sideboard containing "the best wines of Europe."[58] Once Marion and Lee decided that setting the house afire was necessary, it was left to Lee to address Mrs. Motte. Lee informed Rebecca that her mansion must burn:

With a smile of complacency this exemplary lady listened to the embarrassed officer, and gave instant relief to his agitated feelings, by declaring, that she was gratified with the opportunity of contributing to the good of her country, and that she should view the approaching scene with delight. Shortly after, seeing accidentally the bow and arrows which had been prepared, she sent for the lieutenant-colonel, and presenting him with a bow and its apparatus imported from India, she requested

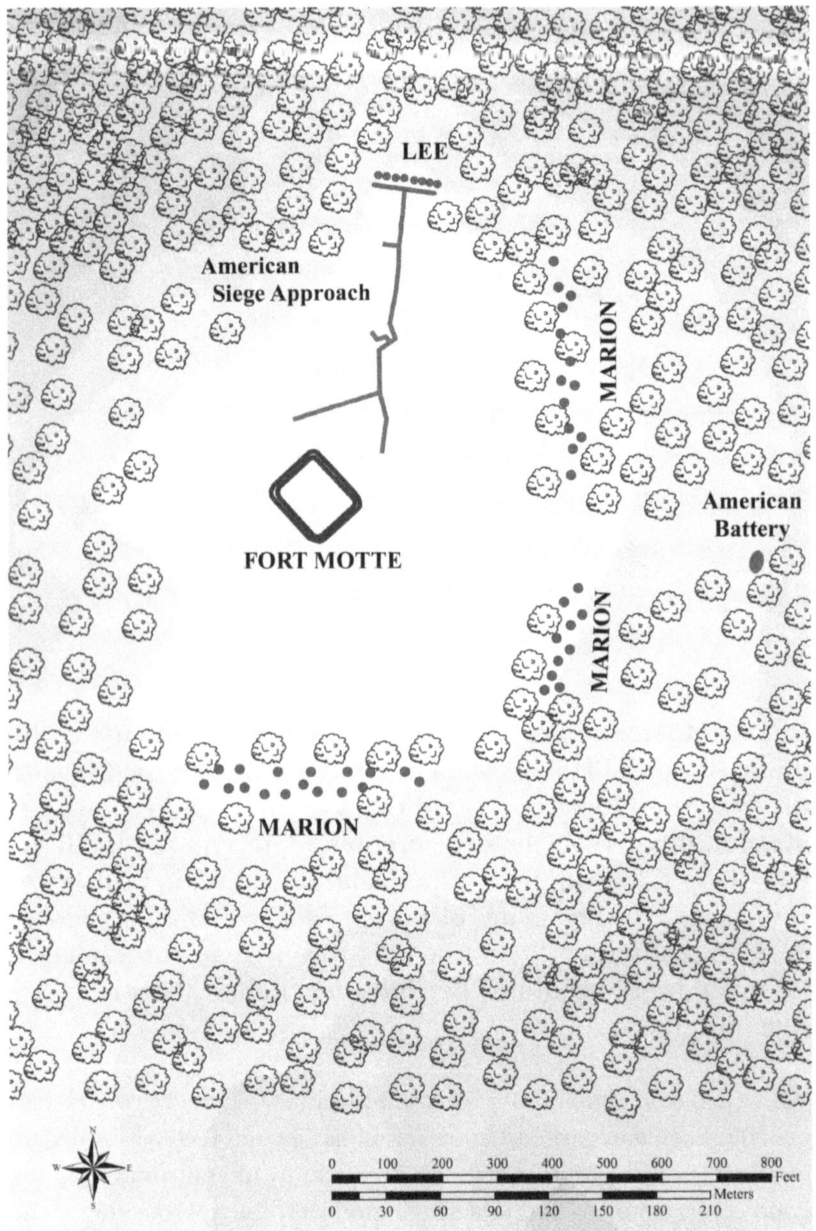

Figure 21. Archaeologist's conception of the last day of the siege of Fort Motte from above. (*Tamara Wilson, courtesy SCIAA*)

his substitution of these, as probably better adapted for the object than those we had provided.[59]

It seems extremely fortuitous that Mrs. Motte would have had a bow and arrow at her farmhouse ready for use (Figure 22). If the bow and arrow were the family heirlooms of Mrs. Motte, why were they not at the mansion? Did Mrs. Motte pick them up as she was leaving the house when the British threw her out? Amazingly, Mrs. Motte's grandson, C. C. Pinckney, claims that that was, in fact, what happened: "These arrows had been brought from the East Indies by a sea captain, and presented to his employer, Miles Brewton, a wealthy merchant of Charleston, and brother of Mrs. Motte . . . the arrows fell into his sister's possession, and were fortunately carried by the ladies, when dismissed from the fort, to their more humble abode."[60] When Lee told Rebecca that the house would burn, she found the arrows on top of her wardrobe and gave them to her daughter to deliver to the soldiers.[61]

A slightly different version is told by Alexander Garden Jr. Garden was the son of a famous naturalist, also named Alexander and a Loyalist. Alexander junior served in Lee's Legion. After the war he published his "anecdotes" of the war, some of dubious accuracy. Nevertheless, Alexander met Mary "Polly" Brewton, after the war. According to Mrs. Brewton, when McPherson threw the family out of the mansion, it was Mrs. Brewton who grabbed the bow and quiver of arrows, stating, "I will take these with me, to prevent their destruction by the soldiers." As she passed out of the gate, McPherson intercepted her and took an arrow; touching the point to his finger, he asked, "what have you here, Mrs. Brewton," to which she returned, "For God's sake, Major, be careful, these arrows are poisoned."[62] Garden's version relates that the first fire arrow shot by the Americans missed the house and fell near McPherson, who picked it up and angerly grumbled, "I thank you, Mrs. Brewton." Later, after the surrender, McPherson confronted Polly, saying "to you, Madam, I owe this disgrace; it would have been more charitable to have allowed me to perish by poison, than to be thus compelled to surrender my post to the enemy."[63]

Figure 22. Mrs. Motte Directing Marion and Lee to Burn Her Mansion. (*John Blake White, before 1859, U.S. Senate*)

Pinckney adds another detail that is independently verified. "The arrows were discharged from a rifle; the two first did not ignite; the third set the roof on fire."[64] More accurately, a smoothbore musket was used to launch the arrows like a mortar.[65] Pinckney's musket arrow version was confirmed by British lieutenant Roderick MacKenzie after the war. MacKenzie wrote a scathing review of Lieutenant Colonel Banastre Tarleton's history of the southern campaigns. In it is a detailed appendix describing the siege of Ninety Six, South Carolina, occupied by the British and besieged by General Greene just a month after Fort Motte was captured. MacKenzie describes how Greene used fire arrows, fired from muskets, against the fortified town of Ninety Six. He adds a footnote explaining:

These were arrows fitted to the bore of musquets from which they were discharged. They were entwined with flax, dipped in combustibles lighted, and armed at the end with a barbed spear. Captain McPherson of Delancey's had defended Fort Motte with admirable gallantry, but his barracks being set on fire by these arrows, he was compelled to surrender.[66]

There are other versions. William Dobein James, perhaps an eyewitness, remembers it differently.[67] He remembers that "This deed of Mrs. Motte has been deservedly celebrated. Her intention to sacrifice her valuable property was patriotic; but the house was not burnt, as is stated by historians, nor was it fired by an arrow from an African bow, as sung by the poet.—Nathan Savage, a private in Marion's brigade, made up a ball of rosin and brimstone, to which he set fire, slung it on the roof of the house."[68]

Savage's sling would seem to be a much harder task than shooting arrows. In order to achieve an uninhibited and accurate throw, Savage probably would have had to climb out of the narrow sap, exposing himself to British fire. Furthermore, the brimstone would have had to be slung at least sixty feet horizontally and twenty feet vertically to get onto the lowest point of the roof.[69] One would assume that this is possible; however it would have been a great feat, where a simpler and safer method was to shoot arrows from the sap.[70]

Adding more intrigue to the story, archaeological evidence suggests that the Americans did indeed abandon their fire arrows in favor of Mrs. Motte's arrows as Lee stated. A fire arrow has been recovered (Figure 23). This fire arrow is 4.38 inches long and consists of an iron nail or rod stock that has been cold-hammered into the shape of an arrow point with a long shank. The tip of the point has been thinned to give it a sharp edge. The shank of the arrowhead would have been inserted into the end of a wooden arrow shaft. Most intriguing is that the arrowpoint was found at the American camp downhill and near the entrance to the sap![71] Had the arrowpoint been found at the fort, it would have demonstrated that fire arrows were being used to set the house on fire. Found near the sap (Figure 13), however, it suggests that the

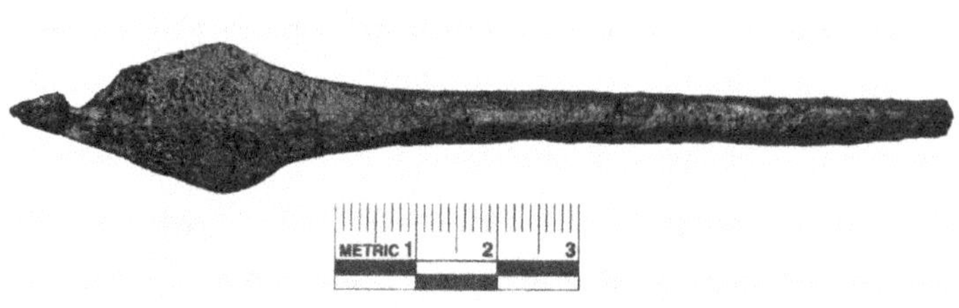

Figure 23. Fire Arrow Recovered by Archaeologists at Sap Camp North and Downhill from Sap Entrance. (*James Legg, courtesy SCIAA*)

Americans tossed it away, in favor of something better, like Mrs. Motte's arrows? For the record, there is yet another legend that Mrs. Motte ordered her slave Cuffe to shoot the arrows rather than Nathan Savage.[72] Francis Rawdon, who was not an eyewitness, but was most assuredly debriefed by eyewitness Captain-Lieutenant Charles McPherson only a few days later, states that the house was ignited using fire arrows.[73] In the final analysis, the best scenario is that the house was set afire by arrows fired from a musket, perhaps by Nathan Savage.

SURRENDER

Lee relates that "The first arrow struck, and communicated its fire; a second was shot at another quarter of the roof, and a third at a third quarter; this last also took effect; and like the first, soon kindled a blaze."[74] McPherson ordered his men up to the roof, but a round or two of canister from the American 6-pounder cannon drove them back down. With the roof burning and the fire endangering the 184 men packed inside the tiny fort, some men panicked and threw themselves over the parapet and breastworks rather than scrambling through the gate.[75]

McPherson hung out the white flag. The Americans immediately joined the British in putting out the fire.

SIX

After the Siege

THE CAPTURE OF FORT MOTTE was a surprisingly bloodless affair, but costly for Marion. As noted in the previous chapter, he lost two sharpshooters. One was one of his bravest men, recently promoted Lieutenant Allen McDonald, who had been with Marion through the fall of 1780 when Marion was alone in the northern part of the state, fighting a partisan war without the support of a conventional army.[1] The other casualty was a Lieutenant Cryer who emulated McDonald.[2] The British lost Corporal Peter Laffon of the 84th Regiment of Foot who was killed on May 8.[3]

The American tally of prisoners was 184 men. The British prisoners included one captain, two lieutenants, two ensigns, one sergeant major, one sergeant, three corporals, one drummer, and sixty-nine privates. The Hessians included one lieutenant, one ensign, five corporals, one drummer, and fifty-one privates.[4] Tories were simply listed as forty-five privates.[5]

Besides the prisoners, the Americans recovered the carronade, "140 stands of arms, a quantity of salt, provisions, and other stores."[6] Lee states that the British regulars surrendered to his Continentals while the Loyalists surrendered to Marion's militia.[7]

It has been noted that clearly there had been a falling out between Marion and Lee during the siege, and perhaps at least part of it involved the treatment of the Loyalist prisoners. Sometime after the surrender, the officers—British and American—retired to Mrs. Motte's old house for a "sumptuous dinner" probably on Buckhead. Mrs. Motte's dinner was "soothing in the sweets of social intercourse the ire which the preceding conflict has engendered." Rebecca was the gracious host to both parties "conversing with ease, vivacity, and good sense, she obliterated our recollection of the injury she had received."[8] During the meal, a British officer was embarrassed by Peter Horry. The officer noted how fortunate it was that Horry had escaped the British at the Sampit Bridge battle in March 1781, since the British had 1,200 men in that engagement. Horry agreed he was fortunate, as he had no idea the British had that many. The captain then noted that he too was fortunate, in that he had hid in the high grass when Marion had surprised the British at Nelson's Ferry back in September 1780. Horry replied, "Truly, you were, . . . for Marion had but 30 militia on that occasion."[9] The next day the British were sent on their way to Lord Rawdon at Nelson's Ferry.[10]

But while the officers were paroled, and the British regulars would be exchanged for American prisoners soon afterward, a different fate awaited the Loyalists. Levi Smith, the commander of the Loyalist troops, left a detailed description of what happened to him and his comrades. Smith, a close neighbor of the Mottes, admits to being a spy for the British—Lord Rawdon "applied to me to provide him intelligence of the movements of Sumter, and other rebel partisans on the western frontier."[11] When Smith's store on the north side of the Congaree was robbed, he moved to a house within two hundred yards of Mrs. Motte's mansion. When the fort was built, McPherson appointed him commander of the Loyalists at the fort, and he was awaiting a formal commission from Lord Rawdon. As mentioned in chapter 5, he was caught by Lee's mounted troops when the Americans arrived on May 6. According to Smith, he was stripped of all but his shirt, and made to run to Colonel Thomson's plantation, where Marion had his headquarters. There, Mrs. Thomson gave him some clothes. The next day a soldier in Marion's command by the name of William Cooper proposed to Marion that Smith be exchanged for Cooper's brother or cousin, Samuel Cooper. Sam had been captured by the British when they raided Marion's Snow's Island supply depot on the Pee Dee in March 1781. Marion agreed and sent a woman to Lord Rawdon to propose the exchange. Unknown at the time to Marion, Cooper, or Smith, when she arrived at Nelson's Ferry, Rawdon thought she was a spy and held her there.

Over the next few days as the siege progressed, the prisoner Smith was treated quite well. William Cooper was Smith's guard, and by day they would go fishing on the Congaree River. Smith was allowed to eat at home but confined each night. The mood, however, changed when the fort was taken. The captured enlisted Loyalists, including Smith, were thrown into Colonel Thomson's millhouse at the base of Mount Joseph hill. On the evening the siege ended, one of Lee's cadets, Francis "little Lee," came and asked for Lieutenant Fulker (or Tulker) of the Loyalists. Fulker had been identified and accused of throwing a "Mrs. Tate" out of her house previously, causing her to catch cold and die. Fulker pleaded for his life but was taken up to the fort and hanged on Mrs. Motte's gatepost.[12] Next, Lee's Continentals came for John Jackson, who was accused of killing one of Sumter's men in Sumter's attack against Belleville. Fulker was cut down and Jackson met the same end.[13] The next morning both Fulker and Jackson were thrown into the fort's ditch, which was being leveled at the time. Then, Hugh Miscally was rousted out of the millhouse, accused of being a guide for the British, probably to Marion's Snow's Island camp.[14] He too was hanged. Then they came for Levi Smith.

Smith was shocked, all the time thinking he was to be soon exchanged for Samuel Cooper. He was accused of being a justice of the peace under the British and an enemy of the state. As they dragged him out of the millhouse, he pleaded for someone to tell his wife and child what was happening. Again, they stripped him of his clothes, except a pair of trousers. As his wife and child watched from a distance, he was about to be hanged when Marion appeared on horseback with his sword drawn:

He asked in a passion, what they were doing here? The soldiers answered, We are hanging them people, Sir! He then asked them, who ordered them to hang any person? They replied Col. Lee. "I will let you know, damn you," replied Marion, "that I command here, and not Col. Lee. Do you know, that if you hang this man, Lord Rawdon will hang a good man in his place; that he will hang Sam. Cooper, who is to be exchanged for him?"[15]

Although saved by Marion, Smith's problems were not over, but eventually General Greene released him and he made his way to Charleston.[16] Although he was most certainly a self-promoter, his account includes vivid details of his terrifying experience. Henry Lee, on the other hand, records a different version of Smith's character:

Among the latter [captured Loyalists] was a Mr. Smith, who had been charged with burning the houses of his neighbors friendly to their country. This man consequently became very obnoxious, and his punishment was loudly demanded by many of the militia serving under the brigadier; but the humanity of Marion could not be overcome. Smith was secured from his surrounding enemies, ready to devote [?] him, and taken under the general's protection.[17]

There is another story that relates to the Loyalist prisoners. According to Joseph Johnson, many of these Loyalists were from German families who had settled in Amelia Township and had established the town of Orangeburg, South Carolina. When Thomson at Belleville heard about the surrender, he rode to Fort Motte and pleaded with Marion and Lee for their release, as he knew the prisoners as neighbors prior to the war and that they had been "compelled to enter the British fort, and made to labor as artificers." Once released, these men hurried away without thanking Thomson. If this happened, it was most likely immediately after the surrender and before the rest were thrown into Thomson's millhouse.[18]

RAWDON'S RETREAT

While Smith, his Loyalists, and the British and Hessians were surrendering to the Americans, certainly they must have wondered where Lord Rawdon was. Unfortunately for them, Rawdon and his command were not marching directly to the relief of Fort Motte. Instead, as related in chapter 5, Lord Rawdon was falling back to the British outpost at Nelson's Ferry downstream. From Lord Rawdon's perspective, the British campaign in South Carolina had reached a particular crisis. With Greene in front of him, Marion and Lee behind, and Lord Cornwallis marching to Virginia, Rawdon was isolated at Camden, cut off from Charleston. Rawdon had indeed wanted to rescue Fort Motte, but marching directly to Fort Motte was out of the question. To get to Marion and Lee he had to first go to Nelson's Ferry where there was a British outpost to protect his crossing with the British forces in Charleston protecting his rear.[19]

Although Rawdon's fires gave hope to the British at Fort Motte, Marion and Lee had little to fear. It would have been difficult for the British to cross the Congaree at McCord's Ferry with Marion and Lee directly on the opposite bank. Rawdon knew he had to make for Nelson's Ferry to cross the Santee. Rawdon reflected on his dilemma in a letter written to Henry Lee, much later, on June 13, 1813. He noted that Colonel Balfour in Charleston was in charge of Forts Motte and Granby, and that he was only concerned with their protection, "an assistance which I had peculiar difficulty in rendering to the two former [Mottes and Granby], from the works having unaccountably been so placed as not to command the ferries, through which blunder succors could not be thrown across the river to the garrisons when invested by an enemy. Hence it happened that on the abandonment of Camden in hope of saving those posts, and protecting the interior country, I was forced to pass the Santee by the circuitous route of Nelson's Ferry."[20]

Rawdon arrived on the north side of Nelson's Ferry on May 13, and upon crossing on the fourteenth he learned that Fort Motte had been lost. "The Stroke was heavy upon me, as all the Provisions had been forwarded from Neilson's [*sic*] to that Post, for the Supply of Camden."[21] The British post at Orangeburg had been taken on May 11 by Sumter. Still, Rawdon was determined to go after Marion and Lee and started up the road to Fort Motte. On the evening of the fifteenth he had made it all the way north to the "point where the road from the Congarees and McCord's Ferry unite."[22] Then his spies reported that Greene had crossed at McCord's Ferry and was making for Orangeburg. This caused him to turn back toward Eutaw Springs. Eventually, he moved farther downstream to camp at Monck's Corner and to ponder his next move. Rawdon's spies were partially correct; Greene had arrived at McCord's Ferry the evening of the surrender, but it was only he and an escort on their way to talk to Marion and Lee. As for the force marching to Orangeburg, the spies had confused Greene with Sumter's small force that has attacked and taken the British post at Orangeburg.[23]

While Rawdon was at Nelson's Ferry on the fourteenth, McPherson and the other officers from Fort Motte arrived, bringing with them the dispatches that had been captured by the Americans when they took Fort Motte. In a war mixed with both terror and honor, the Americans had gentlemanly returned Rawdon's mail, and Lord Rawdon likewise took time to insert a note in a letter to Colonel Lee about the exchange of prisoners, that he "beg leave to return you many thanks for your politeness in transmitting to me the letters which fell into your possession at Motte's house."[24] McPherson also informed Rawdon that Lee had complained that the prisoners from Fort Watson had not complied with their obligations regarding their surrender. Rawdon assured Lee that he would conduct an inquiry. Rawdon destroyed the redoubt at Nelson's Ferry and marched for Monck's Corner.

PRAISE ALL AROUND

When Greene arrived at McCord's Ferry, it was the first time Marion and Greene met face-to-face and possibly the recent exchange about horses came up in their conversations, but with all the good news, perhaps they both decided to let things settle unspoken. In any case, Greene spent the thirteenth and fourteenth at McCord's Ferry writing to the president of the Continental Congress Samuel Huntington of the events of the last few weeks—specifically mentioning Sumter's capture of Orangeburg and Marion and Lee's capture of Fort Motte.[25] He ordered Lee north to capture Fort Granby. Marion was ordered south to move against Georgetown. Both accomplished their missions; Fort Granby fell on May 15, and Georgetown on May 28.

The capture of Fort Motte brought national recognition to Marion and Lee. George Washington issued general orders on June 15, announcing the abandonment of Camden, the capture of Orangeburg, and "the Garrison of Fort Motte consisting of one Captain three Lieutenants three Ensigns, one Serjeant Major, one serjeant eight Corporals, two Drummers and fifers and one hundred and sixty-five privates surrendered prisoners of War to Brigadier General Marion who had carried his approaches to the foot of the Abbatis."[26]

Both the British and Americans praised McPherson for his defense of the fort. Greene called him a "very gallant officer," and Lee wrote "an officer highly and deservedly respected."[27] Nevertheless, Lee also thought McPherson should have been hanged. "Mercy was extended, although policy commanded death, and the obstinacy of McPherson warranted it." For his part, McPherson "frankly acknowledged his dependent situation, and declared his readiness to meet any consequence with the discharge of his duty, conformably to his own conviction of right, might produce."[28]

Lord Rawdon also commended Lieutenant McPherson in writing immediately upon his arrival at Nelson's Ferry, which was published in the June 6, 1781, issue of the *Royal Gazette*:

Rawdon to McPherson, May 14, 1781: Sir, I have just been informed of the misfortune which was befallen you. I lose no time in assuring you that it by no mean diminishes, in my eyes, the merit of your gallant defense.[29]

He followed up later in a letter to Cornwallis, again describing McPherson as "gallant."[30] Shortly afterward, Colonel Balfour, in Charleston issued garrison orders, thanking McPherson and Captain Neil Campbell of the 84th for their "conduct and firmness on the occasion."[31]

Lord Rawdon escaped blame for his part also. General Henry Clinton, in command of all British forces in America, wrote Rawdon that the loss of Forts Motte, Watson, Granby, and Orangeburg "was not, I am fully persuaded, owing to any want of exertion in Your Lordship." Clinton laid the blame on Cornwallis's exposing South Carolina when he moved to Wilmington, an argument with some merit.[32]

The fort itself was destroyed, the ditch filled in, and the palisade torn down. Marion and Lee's "leveling" of the fort was probably haphazard. Adding to the indignity that General Thomas Sumter undoubtedly suffered by failing to take Belleville and Granby, it was he who became responsible for the complete leveling of Forts Motte, Granby, and the Camden fortifications. Sumter had captured Orangeburg on May 11 but hung around until the fifteenth, the day Fort Granby surrendered to Henry Lee. On the sixteenth he sent a letter to Greene begging leave to resign due to what he claimed was discontented militia and his own sickness. Greene rejected his resignation the next day, but in another letter that same day, ordered him to level the fortifications. Sumter, no doubt with much angst, collected twenty slaves from Governor William Bull's plantation to level the works at Motte's. Sumter complied and reported them "Tolerably well Demolished."[33] An archaeological profile of the Fort Motte ditch certainly indicates that it was filled in at different times, as there were several separate stratigraphic levels of fill.

While Benson Lossing says Rebecca's mansion was "desolated" by the fire and that she built another house after the war, William Dobein James said the house was not severely damaged when it caught fire.[34] Apparently, it was repaired and in good enough condition to live in because Rebecca was still there in November 1781. An order from Captain Nathaniel Pendleton to Lieutenant James Simmons was issued on November 9, 1781, to take six dragoons and escort Rebecca from her Congaree home to Fairfield, her plantation on the Santee. At the time, "sculking parties" were prevalent along the Carolina roads and she needed protection.[35] It's possible, however, that she stayed longer. On December 29, the 1st Pennsylvania Regiment, marching southward from Camden, arrived at nearby Thomson's plantation. Lieutenant William Feltman's diary entry for that day records:

> 29th—This morning at sunrise we crossed the Congaree River, and encamped on the south of Col. Thompson's, (a gentleman who lives in great affluence.) Has a very elegant mansion house, which is surrounded by a number of negro houses.
>
> The widow Mot [*sic*] and Mr. Dart live within sight of Col. Thompson's on a very high hill. The situations of both places are very elegant.[36]

This suggests that Rebecca was still there, but on the other hand, Feltman may have been told that it was Rebecca's house in the distance, not that she was there at the time. It is not clear then when exactly Rebecca left Mount Joseph. Certainly, she was at her Fairfield plantation before March 27, when a British raiding party captured a guest named Henry Pendleton, a Charleston judge who had escaped the city when it surrendered. Pendleton had hidden in a rolled-up carpet and was finally found after three searches of the house. The British also ransacked the house, but the commander Major Thomas Fraser made them return some of their plunder.[37]

The reference Feltman made to a Mr. Dart is another mystery. Mrs. Margaret Dart and her children accompanied Rebecca from Fairfield Plantation in 1780 and had been there ever since. Mr. Dart, it is assumed, would have been her husband John Sanford Dart, paymaster in the 1st Regiment and who served in the Jacksonboro Assembly. There is no other mention of him being at Motte's, however. Perhaps Feltman meant Mrs. Dart.

MOUNT JOSEPH, 1781–1796

Being a strategic point along the road between Camden and Charleston, the war continued to pass through the Fort Motte-Belleville area until its end, including the 1st Pennsylvania mentioned above. The most important examples of troop movements in the area, however, were the British and American maneuvers leading up to the Battle of Eutaw Springs. Through much of August 1781, 1,500 British camped at Thomson's plantation, leaving around September first and making for Monck's Corner.[38] If the British had stayed, Belleville might have been the scene of a major battle, for Nathanael Greene was marching to meet the British camped at Thomson's at that time. Greene crossed the river at Howell's Ferry, between Fort Granby and McCord's Ferry, and camped at Motte's (Figure 13).[39] From there they moved toward Eutaw Springs, where eventually they met the British in the last major Revolutionary War engagement in South Carolina.[40]

Although Rebecca was at Fairfield, Mount Joseph was still an active plantation late in the war. A detachment of cavalry under the command of a Lieutenant John Linton had "taken post" at the plantation in March 1783 and was using up all the "produce and provisions." Rebecca's overseer had complained to General Greene and Greene ordered Linton to "make the burden fall as equally upon all the people as possible."[41]

William Thomson's Belleville also returned to normal plantation life and Mrs. Catharine Greene, the General's wife, visited there on her trip to see her husband at Pon Pon, South Carolina, in March of 1782.[42] A Loyalist detachment was reported to have roamed the Belleville neighborhood that September, but it appears nothing occurred.[43]

Rebecca Motte sold the property in September of 1796 to the son-in-law of Colonel William Thomson. By that time, she was living at her El Dorado plantation down along the Santee. Eventually, she and her son-in-law Thomas Pinckney built an impressive mansion there. Pinckney lost his first wife Betsey Motte and married Betsey's sister Frances in 1797.[44]

Epilogue

After the fall of Forts Watson and Motte, and the evacuation of Camden, the British would carry on for another two years and there would be many more battles. After Lee took Fort Granby, he moved against the British post at Augusta, and Greene, with much needed captured supplies from Orangeburg, Motte, and Granby, moved to lay siege to Ninety Six, where Lee would later join him. The siege failed and Rawdon arrived there shortly after Greene abandoned the effort and left. Then Rawdon ordered the post abandoned, and the town burned. The British would never be on the offense again and were confined to the Charleston environs for the rest of the war. The last major land battle in South Carolina occurred on September 8, 1781, at Eutaw Springs, a few miles west of Marion's plantation holdings along the Santee.

Nisbet Balfour, perhaps whistling past the graveyard, downplayed the loss of the posts (Motte, Granby, Augusta, and Fort Watson) in his June 27 report to Lord George Germain:

However, I have the satisfaction to inform your lordship that the stores in them were but inconsiderable and the amount of regular troops in all not exceeding six hundred, and even they have since been exchanged under a cartel which was lately taken place between Lord Cornwallis and Major-General Greene for the release of all prisoners of war in the southern district.[1]

Lord Rawdon better understood the loss of the posts, and Fort Motte in particular, writing Cornwallis: "The stroke was heavy upon me as all the provisions had been forwarded from Neilson's [Nelson's] to that post for the supply of Camden."[2] And for the larger strategic situation, he summed up his part in an earlier letter to Balfour. On May 15 he wrote, "I shall push to Monck's Corner, & shall cause the Post at Neilsons [Nelson's] to be evacuated. The wounded are already moved. I have written to Maxwell [commander at Fort Granby], giving him leave to [?] off if he thinks it necessary. You see, I give up everything to secure the main object."[3] A bitter retort . . . he had given up South Carolina to secure Charleston.

It is worth pausing here then, to consider the significance of the fall of Forts Watson and Motte, and by extension, Orangeburg and Granby. Although these fairly bloodless events were nothing on the grand scale of the American Revolution, together they constitute a turning point in the Southern Campaign. There is no doubt that Rawdon's abandonment of Camden marked the end of the British hold on South Carolina, and that the fall of the forts were instrumental in his decision.

Ironically, after the battle of Hobkirk's Hill, there is evidence that Greene was despondent, thinking the American cause was lost! Reflecting on this critical juncture, Colonel William Davie recorded a conversation he had with Greene in which Greene listed all that was against him, which included: Rawdon's superior force, having pushed Greene back, would now be free to strike Marion and Lee; Rawdon would push Greene to the mountains; Greene's regulars were "reduced to a handful" while the militia was insufficient; Sumter refused to support him; North Carolina was dispirited; and Congress had seemingly abandoned him.[4] Greene, according to Davie, considered leaving the state, quitting the Continentals in South Carolina to take over the American forces in Virginia.[5] Lieutenant Colonel John Eager Howard of the 2nd Maryland Regiment wrote after the war that Greene had Colonel William Washington's horse in "readiness to attend General Greene to Virginia."[6] While Greene was attempting to placate and buck up an angry and despondent Marion, he himself was ready to quit. We have seen just how frustrated Marion was after six years of war, the last year negotiating with an unreliable, fickle militia, and an obnoxious Sumter. Sumter himself was frustrated by Marion's intransigence and success in taking Forts Watson and Motte, and by Lee's capture of Fort Granby, all where he had failed. Indeed, Sumter would also offer his resignation to Greene a few days later.[7]

William Johnson observed in 1822 that:

> Great and sudden were the changes in the aspect of affairs between the 6th and 10th of May. While the prospect remained that Watson would be intercepted, every hope was suspended on that event; as soon as it was ascertained that he had escaped and entered Camden, the deepest gloom for a moment, overspread the public mind. But, sudden and great was the transition from fear to exultation, when Rawdon's retreat was announced. A scene the most busy and bustling imaginable immediately ensued.[8]

Perhaps we can be even more precise and identify May 12, 1781 as that turning point in the American Revolution. On the ninth, Marion and Greene were despondent and frustrated. On May 10, Rawdon abandoned the backcountry, and Cornwallis began his march to Virginia. On May 12, 1781, one year to the day after the fall of Charleston in 1780, Marion and Lee captured Fort Motte (Figure 24).

Figure 24. Fort Motte Today, Facing South Along American Sap with Daughters of the American Revolution Monument in Background. (*James Legg, courtesy of SCIAA*)

Notes

PROLOGUE

1. Francis Marion was born around 1732 in South Carolina. Tradition has it that he gained his partisan skills in the Cherokee campaigns of 1759–1761. William Moultrie described Marion as "an active, brave and hardy soldier." In 1775, he was selected a captain in Moultrie's Second South Carolina Regiment of Infantry and worked his way up through the officer corps, eventually becoming lieutenant colonel and commander of the Second South Carolina Regiment. He participated in the failed siege of Savannah, and due to injury, was released from duty just prior to the fall of Charleston in May 1780. Marion traveled to North Carolina and joined a second Continental Army under Major General Johann Baron De Kalb. When Major General Horatio Gates took command and marched into South Carolina, Marion joined the march. Prior to the Battle of Camden, Marion was detached to take command of the Williamsburg militia.

Arriving on August 17, 1780, at Witherspoon's Ferry (Johnsonville, South Carolina), Marion began his career as a partisan in the northeastern part of the state. In December 1780, Major General Nathanael Greene arrived in South Carolina and Marion and Greene formed a bond that was tested at Fort Motte. At the end of December, South Carolina governor John Rutledge commissioned Marion as a brigadier general in the South Carolina militia, and when Thomas Sumter resigned, Marion became commander of all the South Carolina militia. When the British abandoned Charleston on December 14, 1782, Marion dismissed his militia and returned to the ruins of his Santee River plantation. With his plantation and fortune in ruins, the state made him commandant of Fort Johnson, providing a modest salary. He married Mary Esther Videau, which restored his wealth, but they had no children. He died on February 27, 1795. See Robert Bass, *Swamp Fox, The Life and Campaigns of General Francis Marion* (New York: Henry Holt and Company, 1959); John Oller, *The Swamp Fox: How Francis Marion Saved the American Revolution* (New York: Da Capo Press, 2016); Steven D. Smith, *Francis Marion and the Snow's Island Community* (Asheville, NC: United Artists Press, 2021).

Marion, known as the "Swamp Fox," was the subject of several early nineteenth-century biographies that have shrouded much of what we know about him in myth. The most prominent of these biographies are: Peter Horry and Parson M. L. Weems, *The Life of General Francis Marion: A Celebrated Partisan Officer, in the Revolutionary War, against the British and Tories in South Carolina and Georgia* (Philadelphia, PA: J. B. Lippincott, 1891, original 1809); William Dobein James, *A Sketch of the Life of Brigadier General Francis Marion* (Charleston, SC: Gould and Riley, 1821, reprint Marietta, GA, Continental Book Company, 1948); and William Gilmore Simms, *The Life of Francis Marion* (New York: G. F. Cooledge & Brother, 1844). Today, we think of the "Swamp Fox" as a nom de guerre or sobriquet. Being labeled a swamp fox in colonial times, however, was a pejorative. Swamps were undesirable places. They were unhealthy, dark places—the home of diseases and miasmas. Marion himself saw swamps as generally unnavigable and swamp people undesirable. On September 15, 1780, Marion wrote to Major General Horatio Gates describing a skirmish at Blue Savannah, South Carolina, where Marion chased the Loyalists into the swamps "impassible to all but Tories." Here was Marion, who would be the famed Swamp Fox, deploring Loyalist militia for actions that would make him a national hero!

The nom de guerre first appears as a pejorative in Horry and Weems's biography, where two young ladies being escorted by British officers are fearful that their beaus will be captured by that vile "swamp fox." William Dobein James's biography ascribes the naming of Marion as the Swamp Fox to British lieutenant colonel Banastre Tarleton, who, after unsuccessfully chasing Marion through the swamps, proclaimed, "Come my boys! let us go back, and we will soon find the game cock [Thomas Sumter], but as for this d—d *old fox* [italics in original], the devil himself could not catch him." It was William Gilmore Simms who really turned the curse into a sobriquet, changing 'd——d *old fox*' into 'd——d *Swamp Fox*" [italics and capitalization in the original]. That made Swamp Fox standard in the Marion literature thereafter. Intriguingly, there is some contemporary evidence of Marion as a swamp fox during the American Revolution. In a 1782 Loyalist newspaper, the *Royal Gazette*, the editors published a list of new book titles as a spoof on American leaders like Nathanael Greene and Andrew Pickens and Marion was included. On the list were "A topographical description of the northern parts of South Carolina, betwixt Peedee and Santee, illustrated with a map, wherein are accurately delineated all the thickets and swamps in that country, from an actual survey by Brigadier General Marion," and "Select maneuvers for cavalry; to which are added practical observations on the most soldier-like manner of swimming rivers in a route, by the same." There was also a poem, published in 1829, entitled, "The Swamp Fox," which the editor found in old papers and believed "convey[ed] a good deal of the spirit of the time," implying that it was composed during the revolution. See Marion to General Horatio Gates, September 15, 1780, in, Walter Clark, editor, *Colonial and State Records of North Carolina, Volume XIV* (Goldsboro, NC: Nash Brothers, 1907), 617; *Royal Gazette*, March 13, 1782; "The Swamp Fox," *Southern Literary Gazette*, 1829; Steven D. Smith, "A Spoof on Francis Marion, the Swamp Fox," *Military Collector & Historian* 67, no. 4 (2015): 357–58.

2. James, 106; Watson to Saunders, April 16, 1781, *Saunders Papers*; Watson to ?, undated, Sir Henry Clinton, *Clinton Papers*, William Clements Library [WCL], University of Michigan, Ann Arbor.
3. Francis Marion's Orderly Book, April 1, 1781, Huntington Library, San Marino, California.
4. Watson to ?, undated, Clinton Papers, WCL.
5. Born to a wealthy Rhode Island family in 1742, Nathanael Greene was quickly promoted to brigadier general and then major general early in the war and became a trusted confidant of General Washington. He was in most of the major battles in the northern colonies including Harlem Heights, Trenton, Princeton, Brandywine, Germantown, Monmouth, and Rhode Island. In March 1778, Greene accepted the position of quartermaster general and did an excellent job. After the disastrous Battle of Camden on August 16, 1780, Greene replaced Horatio Gates as commander of the Continental forces in the southern theater, arriving near Charlotte, North Carolina, on December 2, 1781. He reorganized the army and although never won an outright battle, was instrumental in winning the Southern Campaign.

After the war, Greene was rewarded with a two-thousand-acre plantation in Georgia, twelve miles from Savannah, where he settled. He struggled with debt, primarily the result of providing a guaranteed loan for John Banks and Company, which supplied the southern army and resulted in his bankruptcy. Greene died on June 19, 1786, of sunstroke returning home from Savannah. Congress paid off most of his debts in his honor. Kevin Dougherty and Steven D. Smith, *Leading Like the Swamp Fox: The Leadership Lessons of Francis Marion* (Philadelphia, PA: Casemate Books, 2022), 40–43.
6. Charles Cornwallis was born in London on December 31, 1738, to a wealthy and established family. In May of 1761, Cornwallis became a lieutenant colonel of the 12th Regiment of Foot. He volunteered and became a lieutenant general in the British Army in North America in 1776. In the northern campaigns, he distinguished himself at Long Island, Brandywine, Germantown, and Monmouth. He became second-in-command of British forces in North America under Henry Clinton. After Clinton captured Charleston in May 1780, Clinton appointed Cornwallis commander of the British forces in the south. He defeated Major General Horatio Gates at Camden on August 16, 1780, but American partisan victories in the upcountry, including the defeat of Patrick Ferguson's detachment at King's Mountain, South Carolina, and Lieutenant Colonel Banastre Tarleton's defeat at the Battle of Cowpens thwarted Cornwallis's plans. Leaving Lord Francis Rawdon in command of the British field forces in South Carolina, Cornwallis chased Greene across North Carolina without success. Greene and Cornwallis finally met at Guilford Courthouse in a standup fight. Cornwallis was technically the winner, but his army suffered heavily, and he was forced to remove to British-occupied Wilmington, North Carolina.

Still seeking a decisive victory against the Patriots, he decided that the opportunity lay in Virginia, and moved north in April 1781 and eventually was trapped at Yorktown, where he surrendered October 19, 1781. Cornwallis came out of the American rebellion with his reputation untarnished. He returned to England and was greeted as a hero, the blame for the Yorktown fiasco placed on Henry Clinton. Cornwallis was made governor general of India in 1786 and lord lieutenant of Ireland in 1797. Returning to India in 1805 as governor general, he died that same year. See John Buchanan, *The Road To Guilford Courthouse, The American Revolution in the Carolinas* (New York: John Willey & Sons, 1997), 73–75; Hugh F. Rankin, "Charles Lord Cornwallis: Study in Frustration," in *George Washington's Opponents: British Generals in the American Revolution*, ed. George Athan Billias (New York: William Morrow and Company, Inc., 1969), 193–232; John Oliphant, "Cornwallis, Charles," in *Encyclopedia of the American Revolution, Second Edition, Volume 1*, editor in chief Harold E. Selesky (New York: Thomson Gale, 2006), 271–75.

7. Francis Lord Rawdon was born on December 9, 1754. He arrived in America as a lieutenant of the 5th Foot in 1773. He performed well at the Battle of Bunker Hill, Brooklyn, White Plains, Fort Washington, and Fort Clinton, and on June 15, 1778, was made a lieutenant colonel. That year Rawdon took command of the Volunteers of Ireland, a provincial unit, in Philadelphia. He and the Volunteers participated in the siege of Charleston and were detached to Camden afterward, commanding the left flank at the battle of Camden. Cornwallis left Rawdon in command of British field forces in South Carolina in late January 1781 when he marched into North Carolina to catch Major General Nathanael Greene. Greene entered South Carolina after Cornwallis moved into Virginia and Greene fixed Rawdon at Camden, while Marion and Sumter struck his supply line between Camden and Charleston including Fort Watson and Fort Motte, the subjects of this book. After the battle of Hobkirk's Hill he abandoned the village and fell back to Nelson's Ferry. He relieved the besieged British post at Ninety Six, South Carolina, during the hot summer of 1781 but then burned the town and abandoned the backcountry for good. By that time, Rawdon, now ill, resigned and returned to England. His ship was captured by the French, but he was quickly exchanged.

After the war he become a member of the Irish House of Commons. He served some thirty-two years as a politician in the Irish House of Commons and the British House of Lords. In 1812, he was appointed governor general of Bengal and commander of all British forces in India. Rawdon ended his career as governor of Malta in 1824, dying two years later. See Sir Stephen Leslie, "Hastings, Francis Rawdon" in *Dictionary of National Biography*, Volume XXV (London: Elder Smith & Company, 1891), 117–22; Paul David Nelson, "Rawdon-Hastings, Francis," in *Encyclopedia of the American Revolution, Second Edition, Volume 2*, editor in chief Harold E. Selesky (New York: Thomson Gale, 2006), 966–68.

8. Thomas Sumter, the "Gamecock," was an important partisan commander primarily in the backcountry of South Carolina; however, he also attempted attacks against the British depots between Charleston, Ninety Six, and Camden. He was born August 14, 1734, in Hanover County, Virginia. Sumter participated in many early campaigns and battles and was promoted to lieutenant colonel in 1776 and a brigadier general in the militia in the fall of 1780. During the summer and fall of 1780 he engaged the British at Rocky Mount, Hanging Rock, and Fishing Creek. In November 1780, he engaged the British at Fishdam Ford and

at Blackstock. Blackstock may have been Sumter's finest hour. Unfortunately, Sumter was wounded and was out of commission until early in 1781. As will be seen, Sumter was rather recalcitrant and often an irritant to Nathanael Greene.

In February of 1781, Sumter embarked on a raid southward from the back-country attacking the British posts at Fort Granby, Belleville Plantation, and Fort Watson—all failures. Later, he captured the post at Orangeburg while Fort Motte was under siege by Marion and Lee. Sumter proposed, and South Carolina governor John Rutledge agreed, to a scheme to encourage Patriot enlistments, known as "Sumter's Law." The plan was to recruit soldiers by providing clothing, arms, horses, salt, and slaves from Loyalist plantations. General Greene was reluctant and insisted that the Loyalists receive certificates for their seized property. Marion refused to have any part of it. See Anne King Gregorie, *Thomas Sumter* (Columbia, SC: R. L. Bryan Company, 1931); Mathew A. Lockhart, "Sumter, Thomas," in *The South Carolina Encyclopedia*, ed. Walter Edgar (Columbia: The University of South Carolina Press, 2006), 940–41.

9. Rawdon to Cornwallis, March 7, 1781, Ian Saberton, editor, *The Cornwallis Papers: The Campaigns of 1780 and 1781 in the Southern Theatre of the American Revolutionary War, Volume IV* (Uckfield, East Sussex, England: The Naval & Military Press, Ltd, 2010, [hereinafter, Saberton, *CP*, and Vol.]), 49.

10. Hugh Miscally [Maskelly], a guide for Lord Francis Rawdon; lived on Muddy Creek, near Snow's Island. He will play a role in our story of the siege of Fort Motte. There is no direct evidence that he tipped-off Rawdon, but it's a reasonable assumption. Diary of Henry Nase, King's American Regiment, Nase Family Papers, The New Brunswick Museum, transcribed by Todd Braisted; Smith, *Snow's Island*, 131–32, n.100, 142.

11. Walter T. Dornfest, "John Watson Tadwell Watson and the Provincial Light Infantry, 1780–1781," *Journal of the Society for Army Historical Research* 75 (1997): 225.

12. James, 106–7.

13. Henry Lee, known as "Light-Horse Harry," was born into the famous Lee family in Leesylvania, Virginia, in 1756. After a career in the northern theater, Lee was detached to Nathanael Greene's southern command when Greene came south in the fall of 1780. In January 1781, Lee first met Francis Marion when Greene sent the legion into South Carolina and the combined forces attempted to capture Georgetown, South Carolina, but failed. Lee rejoined Greene and his legion played a critical role in the "Race to the Dan" campaign. When Greene moved into South Carolina after the Battle of Guilford Court House, he detached Lee again to join Marion. Their capture of Forts Watson and Motte is the subject of this book. He resigned the army in 1782, feeling underappreciated by Greene. After the revolution, Lee represented Virginia in the United States House of Representatives, was governor, and promoted to general. A poor businessman, he lost all his money and was imprisoned. Attempting to raise funds he wrote his war memoirs, which today is considered unreliable, but often cited. Robert E. Lee, ed., *The Revolutionary War Memoirs of General Henry Lee* (New York: De Capo Press, 1998), 223–25; Oller, 115–17; Charles Royster, "Introduction," in *The Revolutionary War Memoirs of General Henry Lee*, ed. Robert E. Lee (New York: De Capo Press, 1998), iii–iv.

CHAPTER ONE: THE SIEGE AND CAPTURE OF FORT WATSON

1. Watson to ?, undated, Clinton Papers.

2. Watson to ?, undated, Clinton Papers; Watson to Saunders, April 16, 1781, Saunders Papers.

3. Watson to Saunders, April 19, 1781, Saunders Papers.

4. Nisbet Balfour to Charles Cornwallis, April 26, 1781, Saberton, *CP*, Vol. IV, 177.

5. Francis Marion to Nathanael Greene, April 21, 1781, Dennis M. Conrad, editor, *The Papers of Nathanael Greene*, Volume VIII (Chapel Hill: The University of North Carolina Press, 1995 [hereinafter *GP* and Vol. no.]), 128–29; Marion to Greene, April 23, 1781, *GP* VIII, 139; Lee, *Memoirs*, 330. Both dates and locations appear in these documents.

6. Marion wanted to go after Watson, but Lee persuaded him to aim for Fort Watson, more to Greene's orders. See James, 108; Greene to Lee, April 4, 1781, *GP*, Vol. VIII, 46.

7. The road out of Charleston also branched northwest to Dorchester and directly to Orangeburg and Ninety Six.

8. The exact name of this second ferry at this time is problematic. It might have been one of Joseph Manigault's ferries. See https://www.carolana.com/SC/Revolution/revolution_manigaults_ferry_1.html, accessed November 30, 2023. Johnson's map in the *Life of Greene* labels it Sumter's Ferry, which was upstream of Thomas Sumter's plantation, where the road to Nelson's Ferry emerged from Farrar Savannah. See William Johnson, *Sketches of the Life and Correspondence of Nathanael Greene, Volumes I and II* (Charleston, SC: A.E. Miller, 1822). Mill's Atlas indicates that it was called Vance's Ferry in the early nineteenth century. See Robert Mills, *Mills' Atlas of the State of South Carolina* (Greenville, SC: Reprint 1980, Southern Historical Press, Greenville, SC, original 1825).

9. Saberton, *CP*, Vol. II, 199, n.39; Cornwallis to Colonel Banastre Tarleton, December 18, 1780, Saberton, *CP*, Vol. III, 352; Watson, John W. T., undated letter to ?, Clinton Papers. Born in 1748, John Watson Tadwell Watson began his military career as an ensign in the 3rd Regiment of Foot Guards in 1767. He rose in the ranks to lieutenant colonel in the army by 1778. Watson latched on to Henry Clinton in New York and performed well. Asked by Clinton what he could do for him, Watson requested assignment in the South. Clinton created the Provincial Light Infantry for him. The unit sailed south as part of Major General Alexander Leslie's reinforcement to Cornwallis, arriving in Charleston in December 1780. There he was given the independent command to guard the roads to Camden and watch over the northeastern part of South Carolina.

Watson would leave South Carolina in July of 1781 and return to New York. After the war he was eventually promoted to general in 1808. He died in France in 1826. According to Saberton, Watson was arrogant and "reluctant to obey or cooperate with ranking officers whom he considered his professional inferiors (such as Rawdon, Balfour, and Tarleton)." Watson and the light infantry were seen in such poor light that when Cornwallis decided to march into North Carolina he warned Lord Rawdon to act with "great caution," perhaps even to "suffer insults east of Santee, taking great care that Watson may not receive a check," which he thought "but too probable." Cornwallis to Tarleton, December 18, 1780, Saberton, *CP*, Vol. III, 352. There may have been another reason why he was unpopular. As noted, Watson had attached himself to General Clinton and was one of Clinton's favorites. Cornwallis and Clinton were friends early in the war, but the relationship became increasingly strained when Clinton left Cornwallis in South Carolina and Cornwallis began operating on his own. After the war, England blamed Clinton for Cornwallis's surrender at Yorktown and Clinton spent years attempting to change that narrative. See Walter T. Dornfest, *Military Loyalists of the American Revolution, 1775–1783* (Jefferson, NC: McFarland & Company, Inc. 2011), 353; Walter T. Dornfest, "John Watson Tadwell Watson and the Provincial Light Infantry, 1780–1781," *The Journal of the Society for Army Historical Research* (1997).

10. Watson to ?, undated, Clinton Papers.

11. The mound is now within the Santee National Wildlife Refuge and managed by the U.S. Fish and Wildlife Service. University of South Carolina archaeologist Leland Ferguson excavated the site in the 1970s. See Leland Ferguson, *Archeology at Scott's Lake: Exploratory Research 1972, 1973* (Columbia: Research Manuscript Series, South Carolina Institute of Archaeology and Anthropology, 1975); Leland G. Ferguson, "An Archeological-Historical Analysis of Fort Watson: December 1780–April 1781" in Stanley South, ed., *Research Strategies in Historical Archeology* (New York: Academic Press, 1977), 41–71. Ferguson measured its height to be twenty-three feet above the surrounding surface. Marion claimed it was forty feet high, and while it is likely that there has been some erosion, archaeological evidence of the British occupation still existed in 1974 so it is unlikely that it had eroded as much as seventeen feet. See Marion to Greene, April 23, 1781, *GP* VIII, 139. Colonel Henry Lee described it as thirty feet high, Lee *Memoirs*, 332.

12. Ferguson, 1975, 31.

13. This ditch appears to have been dug prior to the attack and deepened during the siege.

14. Watson letter to ?, Clinton Papers.

15. Marion to Greene, April 23, 1781, *GP* VIII, 139.

16. Ferguson 1975, 40.

17. Archaeologist Leland Ferguson found ceramics within the fort indicating that the officers probably used the interior of the fort as their headquarters prior to the blockade and siege. In the field, officers would usually take up quarters in a local plantation house away from the troops, so, absent such a homestead at Fort Watson, this interpretation is most likely correct. Certainly, the fort was too small for continual occupation by the whole detachment, as the British learned during the siege.

18. Thomas Sumter had attempted to attack the British post at William Thomson's plantation, called Belleville, on the Congaree River in February 1781. See chapter 4. The attack was a failure, and he withdrew his force to Manigault's Ferry on the western bank of the Santee north of Fort Watson. There he learned of a supply convoy from Charleston moving up the Charleston to Camden road.

About a mile south of the ferry he attacked the convoy, killing thirteen soldiers, capturing sixty-six, and most importantly, obtaining twenty supply wagons. Shortly after the battle, Sumter learned of the approach of a British relief force. Instead of retreating northward, he decided to put the captured supplies on barges and float them downstream toward Fort Watson, his next target. Unfortunately, the man Sumter hired to guide the barges downstream was a Loyalist. Approaching Fort Watson, the guide promptly steered the barges to the British where they overcame Sumter's guards and reclaimed their supplies. A frustrated Sumter made a brief attack on a British foraging party near the fort on February 28 and then withdrew north. Terry W. Lipscomb, *Names In South Carolina,* Volume XXIV (on file, South Caroliniana Library, University of South Carolina), 16–17; Terry W. Lipscomb, *Revolutionary Battles, Skirmishes, and Actions in South Carolina* (Columbia: The South Carolina American Revolution Bicentennial Commission, n.d.); Edward McCrady, *The History of South Carolina in the Revolution, 1780–1783* (New York: Macmillan and Company, 1902), 107–8.

19. McKay had been wounded as an enlisted man at the battle of Quebec during the French and Indian War and was a well-respected officer. He was detached to Watson's Provincial Light Infantry while at Fort Watson. Not much more is known of him except he was a captain in the Reay Fencibles in 1794. Lawrence Babits, "Perhaps the Most Important Victory of the Whole War," book manuscript in press; Dornfest, *Military Loyalists,* 277.

20. This accounting of McKay's command comes from a prisoner list attached to Marion's letter to Greene, April 23, 1781, *Papers of the Continental Congress,* Item 155, Vol. 1, 171. The officers included a surgeon of the King's American Regiment by the name of Campbell, an Ensign Robinson from the Loyal American Regiment, a Lieutenant Lewis, and Ensign G. M. McKallam from the South Carolina Rangers. Soldiers are listed as "73 British soldiers and 36 Tories." McKay's journal of the siege indicates that some of the British were also from the 64th Regiment of Foot, probably ill or unfit for duty. The Provincial Light Infantry (Watson's unit) is sometimes mentioned as being there also.

Usually, the number of men involved and casualties in American Revolution battles are nearly impossible to know with any reliability. Sources almost always contradict for multiple reasons beyond opposing forces wanting to hide their losses or exaggerate their victories. Men may be present but ill on the day of the battle. Men may desert during the battle. Wounded may hide or crawl off the battlefield. Militia numbers are the least reliable. Militia on both sides came and went without notice depending on the fortunes of war. Marion regularly lost men on the march and gained men when events favored the Americans. Slaves and women involved are almost never mentioned or counted among the troops or as casualties. Readers should never assume the numbers of soldiers involved or casualty lists presented in historical records are exact, even in the primary sources, Fort Watson being an excellent example.

21. Lieutenant James MacKay, *Journal,* printed in full in Ferguson, 1975, 43–44, also in Subject File H-2-5, S.C. Department of Archives and History, Clinton Papers, 9915; 1–4.

22. McKay's Journal. It is impossible to know precisely what McKay means by

"front" and "left." The fort was situated just north of Scott's Lake. To the west was the Santee and likely a swamp. Therefore, the Americans are unlikely to have attacked from either the south or the west. Marion and Lee's initial attack most likely came from the east, with the flankers coming out of the woods from the north, or "left" of his eastern "front." Also, the fort's entrance was in the southeast corner of the fort. It's reasonable to assume that McKay considered the gate as his front.

23. McKay's Journal; Henry Lee to McKay, April 22, 1781, Lee Family Papers, Robert Alonzo Brock Collection, Huntington Library, San Marino, CA.

24. Marion to Greene, April 23, 1781, *GP* VIII, 140.

25. McKay's Journal.

26. Ibid. This well probably was at the base of the mound below the southeastern gate, just inside the outer row of abatis.

27. The difference being that in a blockade those on the outside merely blocked access and egress, while a siege means an attempt to take the fort through offensive action. McKay may have felt that he was under a blockade with so little progress being made by the Americans.

28. Lee to Greene, April 18, 1781, *GP* VIII, 113.

29. McKay's Journal. Marion wrote Greene on April 23 that they did not have entrenching tools and the lack thereof made them eventually turn to the famous tower described below. Marion to Greene April 23, 1781, *GP* VIII, 140. Both Lee and William James also stated that they did not have entrenching tools. James, 109; Lee, *Memoirs*, 332. Leland Ferguson suggests that perhaps the Americans did not have enough tools to get the job done quickly, see Ferguson 1975, 58. This makes sense, because McKay would continue to record the slow progress of the American entrenchments.

30. Greene to Lee, April 19, 1781, *GP* VIII, 117–118.

31. McKay's Journal.

32. Lee to Greene, April 20, 1781, *GP* VIII, 124; Lee to Greene, April 20, 10 PM, *GP* VIII, 125.

33. William Moultrie to Francis Marion, April 16, 1781, in Robert W. Gibbes, *Documentary History of the American Revolution, Volume I* (Columbia, SC: Banner Steam-Power Press, 1853), 52. Born in Dunbog in 1743, Nisbet Balfour started his military career as an ensign in 1761. He took part in many northern battles including the battles of Bunker Hill, Long Island, Brandywine, and Germantown. He was promoted to lieutenant colonel in 1778 in the 23rd Regiment. He came south with Clinton and Cornwallis and was first sent to Ninety Six where he raised many Loyalist recruits and then returned to Charleston. There he was appointed commandant of the British garrison in Charleston and was also responsible for the British forces in the region south of the Santee and Congaree, an area that included Fort Watson and Fort Motte. After the war he was made an aide de camp to the king and served sixty-two years in the service. He rose in the ranks to a full general in 1803. He died at home in Dunbog in 1823. Mark M. Boatner, *Encyclopedia of the American Revolution* (Mechanicsburg, PA: Stackpole Books, 1994, original 1966), 56–57; Leslie Stephen, editor, *Oxford Dictionary of National Biography*, Volume III (London: Smith, Elder, & Co., 1885), 56–57.

34. Oller, 305, note to page 148.
35. Snipes would eventually meet his match against the British who surprised him at his plantation in June 1781. He fought no more, which did not displease Marion. Oller, 171.
36. Peter Horry to Greene, *GP* VIII, 123.
37. See, Bass, *Swamp Fox*, 171–75; Oller, 148–49.
38. Marion to Greene, April 21, 1781, *GP* VIII, 128–29.
39. John James, Audited Account 3993, Accounts Audited of Claims Growing out of the Revolution in South Carolina, 1775–1856, South Carolina Department of Archives and History, Columbia, SC.
40. Colonel William Harden to Marion, April 18, 1781, in Gibbes, *Documentary History, Vol. I,* 54.
41. Gregorie, 137.
42. McKay's journal. Besides the soldiers, this indicates that there were noncombatants in the fort, probably slaves.
43. What the tower looked like exactly is a mystery. Usually, it is depicted as a simple square crib with notched logs placed on top of one another like a classic log cabin (see Figure 6). This would have worked. However, McKay described it as a "Wooden Machine" (McKay's Journal). Being an eighteenth-century professional soldier, he must have used the word to describe a siege machine, something mobile that the Americans "brought down," as in transported to near the fort. The machine could either have been rolled in place using logs or perhaps the foundation was on a wagon. This theory is supported by Lee's account (*Memoirs*, 332) describing the tower as "oblong," that is, rectangular, and a pension application by John Walden that states that the machine consisted of "moving batteries made of moss and Cow's hides," P.A. W9878, and Nathaniel Whittington describing it as a "rolling battery," S9527.

Once set in place, the Americans raised a scaffolding to reach the fort height. This upper section probably consisted of the crib logs. At the top was a row of logs forming a floor and timber wall on the side facing the fort to protect Marion's riflemen. See Lee, 332. The height of the tower is another mystery but interesting to speculate upon. McKay indicates that it was "nearly level with the top of our Works" (McKay's journal). Marion agrees, saying that it was "equal to the heighth [*sic*] of the fort" (Marion to Greene, April 21, 1781, *GP* VIII, 128–29). Lee, however, states that it was high enough that the riflemen had "thorough command of every part of the fort, from the relative supereminence of the tower." See Lee, *Memoirs*, 332. Leland Ferguson's archaeological analysis of the distribution of fired shot within the fort indicates that most of the shot was found along the eastern and southern walls. This is important for two reasons. First, he concludes that the tower must have been located northwest of the fort. Second, in order for the shot to be there, the Americans would have had to fire in a downward angle from their tower as Lee describes. This is supported by the fact that McKay ordered his men to build a traverse across the middle of the fort to hide behind.

This then gives us a clue as to the distance between the fort and the tower. The mound is 130 feet across. It is 23 feet high. Ferguson's excavations revealed what appears to be part of the abatis ditch 40 feet from the base of the mound. The fort's stockade probably did not have to be any higher than 6 feet since anyone not in a tower would have to fire upward from the ground below the mound. Thus, the minimum height of the tower would have to have been 29 feet if the riflemen were lying down and it was next to the fort. If standing, we could subtract around 4 feet for a tower of 25 feet high and a 4-foot wall for the riflemen to hide behind. That height, however, would only allow the Americans to fire parallel along the top of the stockade. In order to fire into the fort, command the inside, and for lead shot to hit near the inside bottom of the opposite wall as seen in the lead shot distributions, one would have to fire downward. If it was right next to the mound, a soldier would have to be able to fire his weapon downward from a height of around 33 or 34 feet. As the distance from the fort increases, the angle of fire into the fort increases and the required height of the tower increases. If it was just outside the outer abatis or 40 feet from the base of the mound, a soldier still would have to level his arm at a height of around 39 feet! It would appear that the tower was around 35 feet in height, assuming a 4-foot protective wall. Perhaps this is why Marion reported that the mound was 40 feet high.

44. Lee, Summons of Fort Watson, April 22, 1781, Lee Family Papers, Huntington Library. Although McKay had the high ground tactically, Lee sought the high ground morally, noting that his summons "was dictated by that spirit of humanity which uniformly regulates the conduct of the American officers."

45. McDonald is most likely the oft mentioned, formerly Sergeant Allen McDonald, a sharpshooter in Marion's forces at many battles. He may have been among those who attacked the Spring Hill Redoubt in the siege of Savannah and was the McDonald who stabbed Loyalist Ganey in the back in a running battle on horseback near Georgetown, South Carolina, and dropped British lieutenant George Torriano with a shot to the leg from three hundred yards in Watson's campaign against Marion. See Bass, *Swamp Fox*, 26, 121, and 150. Marion biographer, John Oller, also says he was among the Maryland Continentals Marion rescued at the raid on a British prisoner detachment at Great Savannah after they had been captured at the Battle of Camden in August 1780. If so, he can't be the same McDonald who was at Savannah. Oller, 78. Patrick O'Kelley believes that Couterier is John Coutirice, a captain in Colonel Richardson's militia in 1775 and later a dragoon. Patrick O'Kelley, *Unwaried Patience and Fortitude: Francis Marion's Orderly Book* (West Conshohocken, PA: Infinity Publishing Company, 2006), 699.

46. Marion to Greene, April 23, 1781, Gibbes, *Documentary History, Vol. I,* 57; Lee 332.

47. Mckay's Journal with articles of capitulation attached.

48. As usual, casualty reports are conflicting. James reports 114 captured while Edward McCrady says 120. McCrady, 748. Marion reported two militia killed and three of Lee's soldiers wounded, but that tally does not agree with McKay's journal, Marion to Greene, *GP* VIII, 140. The fate of the prisoners was noted in Peter Dubose's and John Brumfield's pension applications P.A. S21163, and P.A. S30894.

CHAPTER TWO: SEARCHING FOR WATSON

1 Keystone reference from Larry Babits, "Hobkirk's Hill," in *Encyclopedia of the American Revolution, Volume 1*, editor in chief Harold E. Selesky (New York: Thomson Gale Corporation, Second Edition, 2006), 508.
2. Greene to Samuel Huntington, April 22, 1781, *GP* VIII, 131.
3. Greene to Lee, April 24 and Greene to Marion, April 24, *GP* VIII, 143 to 145.
4. The deserter was a drummer from the Maryland Continentals who had been captured by the British and joined them only to be rescued by Marion and Lee at Fort Watson. He promptly made his way north, rejoined his Continental unit, then deserted again to the British in Camden. See, Boatner, 504.
5. See Babits, "Hobkirk's Hill," and for a recent interpretation, John Buchanan, *The Road to Charleston: Nathanael Greene and the American Revolution* (Charlottesville: University of Virginia Press, 2019), chapter 3.
6. Marion to Greene, April 25, 1781, *GP* VIII, 146–47.
7. Greene to Marion, April 27, 1781, *GP* VIII, 161.
8. Lee to Greene, May 2, 1781, *GP* VIII, 192, n.5. It is not clear to the author if Finley's first name was Ebenezer or Samuel. The editors of the Greene papers names him Ebenezer at the Fort Motte siege. This same detachment follows Lee to Fort Granby. When they get to Fort Grierson's siege on May 25, they name him Samuel. See *GP*, Vol. VIII, 251, 264, 311; Lawrence Babits names him Ebenezer, while Hugh F. Rankin names him Samuel. See Lawrence E. Babits, "Perhaps the Most Important Victory of the Whole War," draft manuscript in press, and Hugh F. Rankin, *The North Carolina Continentals* (Chapel Hill: University of North Carolina Press, 2005, original 1971), 302.
9. See correspondence between Eaton and Greene and notes, *GP*, VIII, 50–51, 106.
10. Marion to Greene, April 27, 1781, *GP* VIII, 163.
11. Marion to Greene, April 30, 1781, *GP* VIII, 179.
12. Lee to Greene, April 27, 1781, *GP* VIII, 163.
13. Lee to Greene, April 30, 1781, *GP* VIII, 178.
14. Alexander Gregg, *History of the Old Cheraws*. (New York: Richardson and Company, 1867), 360–62. Evan Pugh, a minister of the Welsh Neck Baptist Church, noted in his diary on May 4, 1781, that "all ye [the] Men came home from Ge Marion Camp." These may have been Ervin's men or another example of Marion's men leaving to attend to crops. Horace Fraser Rudisill, transcriber, *The Diaries of Evan Pugh (1762–1801)* (Florence, SC: St. David's Society, 1993), 206.
15. Lee to Greene, May 2, 1781, GP VIII, 192.
16. William Johnson states that the reason Marion and Lee missed Watson was due to Eaton's delay in joining Marion with the artillery. "Had he [Eaton] pursued his orders, he must have joined Marion before the receipt of the letter of the 27th, ordering him across the Santee; and by immediately compiling with that order, Marion must have intercepted Watson." William Johnson, *Sketches*, 104.
17. Diary of Henry Nase, entry May 7, 1781. Letter from Captain-Lieutenant Charles McPherson to ? probably Major Andrew Maxwell at Fort Granby, May 5, 1781, author's collection; Watson's Letter, Clinton Papers.

18. Cornwallis to Phillips, April 10, 1781, Saberton, *CP* IV, 114–15.
19. Cornwallis to Balfour, April 22, 1781, Saberton, *CP* IV, 122.
20. Rawdon to Cornwallis, May 24, 1781, Saberton, *CP* V, 288–89.
21. Greene to Marion May 4, 1781, *GP* VIII, 198.
22. Lee to Greene, May 6, 1781, *GP* VIII, 214.

CHAPTER THREE: THE MOTTES AND MOUNT JOSEPH

1. Walter B. Edgar and N. Louise Bailey, *Biographical Directory of the South Carolina House of Representatives, Volume II: Commons House of Assembly 1692–1775* (Columbia: University of South Carolina Press, 1977), 95–97.
2. Ibid., 96. Several accounts relating to Fort Motte state that Miles Brewton obtained Mount Joseph Plantation through his marriage to Mary Izard on May 19, 1759. See for instance, Richard N. Cote, *Mary's World: Love, War, and Family Ties in Nineteenth Century Charleston* (Mount Pleasant, SC: Corinthian Books, 2001), 16. However, the author found no record that the Izard family, who owned some of the largest plantations along the Ashley River near Charleston, ever owned land along the Congaree River. For Izard land holdings see Langdon Cheves, "Izard of South Carolina," *South Carolina Historical and Genealogical Magazine* 2, no. 3 (1901), 205–40 [hereinafter *SCHGM*]; Henry A. M. Smith, "The Upper Ashley; and the Mutations of Families," *SCHGM* XX, no. 3 (1919), 151–98.
3. Cote, 16; Alexander Salley, "Col. Miles Brewton and Some of His Descendants," *SCHGM* 20, no. 1 (1901), 130–31, 142–44, 148–50.
4. Margaret F. Pickett, *Rebecca Brewton Motte: American Patriot and Successful Rice Planter* (Charleston, SC: Evening Post Books, 2022), 11.
5. Ibid., 18–19.
6. Edgar and Bailey, 480–81.
7. Bennett Baxley editor, *St James-Santee Parish Historical Sketches: Plantations, Churches, Villages, and Homes* (St. James- Santee Parish Historical Society, 1997); Anne B. L. Bridges and Roy Williams, III, *St James Santee Plantation Parish: History and Records, 1685–1925* (Spartanburg, SC: The Reprint Company, 1996) 56; Elise Pinckney, "Letters of Eliza Lucas Pinckney, 1768–1782," *SCHGM* 76, no. 3 (1975):145, 165.
8. Pickett, 28.
9. Alexia Jones Helsley, *South Carolinians in the War for American Independence* (Columbia: South Carolina Department of Archives and History, 2000), 65–69.
10. Pickett, 51.
11. Ibid., 53, 57.
12. Francis Leigh Williams, *A Founding Family: The Pinckneys of South Carolina* (New York: Harcourt Brace Jovanovich, 1978), 22, 53, 87.
13. Ibid., 102, 128, 133.
14. Mrs. O.J. Weslin and Miss Agnes Irwin, *Worthy Women of Our First Century* (Philadelphia: J. B. Lippenwith Co., 1877), 264.
15. Margaret Hayne Harrison, *A Charleston Album* (Ringe, NH: Richard R. Smith Publications, Inc., 1953), 36–43.
16. Bass, *Swamp Fox*, 10.

17. Harrison, 38–39.
18. This is based on a letter from Thomas Pinckney stationed at Fort Moultrie to his sister Harriot Pinckney Horry at their Hampton Plantation, dated April 12, 1780. In it he refers to letters addressed to Mr. Motte at nearby Fairfield Plantation, which Pinckney was forwarding. See The Papers of Eliza Lucas Pinckney and Harriott Pinckney Horry, digital edition, https://rotunda.upress.virginia.edu/PinckneyHorry/elp-details.xqy?letter=/PinckneyHorry/ELP0556.xml&return=toc_chron, accessed December 16, 2022 [hereinafter *PELP*].
19. Pickett, 62. Mary was the widow of John Brewton, son of Robert Brewton, Rebecca's half- brother. John had died in 1777.
20. Pickett, 64.
21. Pickett, 68–69. The whereabouts of Jacob Motte are confused. Pickett notes that in a letter from Eliza Pinckney to Betsey Pinckney on June 18, 1780, she mentions that her father, Jacob, was at Hampton Plantation. Yet Nisbet Balfour mentioned Jacob in a letter to Lord Cornwallis on June 6, 1780, which suggests that Jacob was at Buckhead, that is, Mount Joseph. See chapter 4.
22. There is confusion in the historic record as to what contemporaries actually meant by Buckhead. Today, Buckhead refers to the hill along the Congaree River at the confluence of Buckhead Creek north of the hill where Rebecca Motte built her mansion called Mount Joseph. This seems to be the consensus of historic documents pertaining to Rebecca Motte. In looking at pension accounts, however, sometimes the "fort" at Buckhead refers to Thomson's Belleville Plantation, while others refer to Fort Motte or Mount Joseph. Some even confuse Thomson's with Fort Motte. Joseph Gaston's widow, for example, states that he went to "the Siege at Fort Motte commonly called Thompson's." Joseph Gaston W23089. Whether pensioners were actually involved in the siege of Fort Motte or the siege at Belleville must be assumed by who commanded (Marion, Lee, Sumter) and when they think they participated. Even then it's not often clear.
23. Charleston Deed Book B-4, 342–46, recorded February 19, 1773. Charleston Deed Books, South Carolina Department of Archives and History, Columbia, SC.
24. Ibid.
25. Ibid.
26. Will of Miles Brewton, July 16, 1773, Probate Court Book 1774–1782, 298, South Carolina Department of Archives and History, Columbia, SC.
27. *Names in South Carolina*, Volume XII (on file, South Caroliniana Library, University of South Carolina, 1965), 45–46.
28. "Overseers" house is the term used by William James, *A Sketch*, 120. "Farm house" is the term used by Henry Lee, *Memoirs*, 345, and by Benson Lossing in his *Pictorial Field-Book of the Revolution*, original 1850, 2004 edition edited by Jack E. Fryar Jr., (Wilmington, NC: Dram Tree Books, Inc.), 150. Bass uses the term "old log cabin." Bass, *Swamp Fox*, 189.
29. Historian Richard Watkins is credited for this conclusion, which is strongly supported by archaeological investigations indicating a mid-eighteenth-century house site there based on the recovered ceramics. See Steven D. Smith, James

B. Legg, Tamara S. Wilson, and Jonathan Leader, *"Obstinate and Strong": The History and Archaeology of the Siege of Fort Motte* (Columbia: South Carolina Institute of Archaeology and Anthropology, 2007), 59–60.
30. Eliza was the mother of Betsey's husband Thomas Pinckney. Eliza Lucas Pinckney to Elizabeth Motte, June 18, 1780, *PELP* accessed December 19, 2022.
31. Elizabeth Motte to Eliza Lucas Pinckney, July 17, 1780, *PELP* accessed December 19, 2022.
32. Williams, 161.
33. Williams, 169; Thomas Pinckney, Letter to ?, July 31, 1822, Thomas Pinckney Papers, South Caroliniana Library, University of South Carolina.
34. Thomas Pinckney to Horatio Gates, August 18, 1780, *The Papers of the Revolutionary Era Pinckney Statesmen Digital Edition*, ed. Constance B. Schulz. Charlottesville: University of Virginia Press, Rotunda, 2016, https://rotunda.upress.virginia.edu/founders/PNKY-01-01-02-0007-0030 [hererineafter *Papers of Pinckney*].
35. Tarleton was reputed to be a butcher, but in this case, he acted with humanity and also offered to give back Rebecca Motte's horses, which he had seized for his Legion. See Charles Cotesworth Pinckney, *Life of General Thomas Pinckney* (Boston: Houghton, Mifflin and Company, 1895), 80.
36. Banastre Tarleton to Thomas Pinckney, September 2, 1780, in *Papers of Pinkney*. Tarleton ended his letter noting that "I don't mean to be all Profession, but you will always find me happy to contribute to your Ease & Satisfaction as much as lyes within my power."
37. Thomas Pinckney to Harriott Pinckney Horry, September 7, 1780, *PELP*.
38. Harriott Pinckney Horry to Thomas Pinckney, September ? 1780, *PELP*.
39. Eliza Lucas Pinckney to Thomas Pinckney, September 17, 1780, *PELP*.
40. Thomas Pinckney to John Money, September 22, 1780; Money to Pinckney, September 24, *Papers of Pinckney*.
41. Thomas Pinckney to Harriott Pinckney Horry, September 26, 1780, *PELP*. According to Frances Leigh Williams, Pinckney was picked up by Mrs. Robert Brewton in an open cart, *A Founding Family*, 170; Pickett, 82–83.
42. Pickett, 83.
43. Ibid., 86–87.
44. Thomas Pinckney to Eliza Lucas Pinckney, December 6, 1780, *Papers of Pinckney*. Pickett, 87–88.
45. Pickett, 87.
46. Thomas Pinckney to Harriott Pinckney Horry, January 15, 1781, *PELP*.
47. Eventually, he would enter Charleston with the American army when it was abandoned by the British in 1782. He would become governor of South Carolina after the war. See Williams, 174, 182, 183, 191.
48. Pickett, 90.

CHAPTER FOUR: BRITISH IN THE NEIGHBORHOOD

1. Edgar and Bailey, 669–71.
2. Saberton, *CP*, Vol. I, 32.
3. Balfour to Cornwallis, June 6, 1780, Saberton, *CP*, Vol. I, 75. Balfour to Cornwallis, June 7, 1780, Saberton, *CP*, Vol. I, 78.

4. A. S. Salley, *The History of Orangeburg County, South Carolina* (Orangeburg, SC: R. Lewis Berry Printer, 1898), 377.
5. Nisbet Balfour to Lord Cornwallis, June 7, 1780, Saberton, *CP*, Vol. I, 78–79; Balfour to Cornwallis, June 14, 1780, Saberton, *CP*, Vol. I, 90; Diary of Lieut. Anthony Allaire, in Lyman C. Draper, *King's Mountain and its Heroes* (Cincinnati, OH: Peter G. Thomson, 1881), 497; Wade S. Kolb III and Robert M. Weir, *Captured at Kings Mountain: The Journal of Uzal Johnson* (Columbia: University of South Carolina Press, 2011), 18.
6. Balfour to Cornwallis, June 7, 1780, Saberton, *CP*, Vol I, 78–79.
7. Balfour to Cornwallis, June 9, 1780, Saberton, *CP*, Vol. I, 81.
8. Cornwallis to Balfour, June 11, 1780, Saberton, *CP*, Vol. I, 82.
9. Balfour to Cornwallis, June 6 1780, Saberton, *CP*, Vol. I, 74–77 and notes.
10. Probably Major Colin Graham, who was organizing the Royal Orangeburg militia. Saberton, *CP*, Vol. 1, n.81; Cornwallis to Balfour, June 20, 1780, Saberton, *CP*, Vol. I, 98.
11. Lieutenant Colonel Alex Innes to Cornwallis, July 24, 1780, Saberton, *CP*, Vol. I, 266. "[T]here were a knot of vilains [*sic*] that I saw yesterday with Rebel caps in Thomson's piazza that would incline me to cleanse that nest if I had time."
12. Fisher to Haldane?, August 25, 1780, Saberton, *CP*, Vol. II, 329. John Fisher was commissioned that summer as a colonel in the Orangeburg Regiment. He owned over three thousand acres of land in that district prior to the war and was sheriff. After the war he remained in Orangeburg County. Ian Saberton, "Biographical Sketches of Royal Militia Commanders In The South Carolina Mid-and Lowcountry, North Carolina, and Georgia, 1780–82" https://allthingsliberty.com/2020/12/biographical-sketches-of-royal-militia-commanders-in-the-south-carolina-mid-and-lowcountry-north-carolina-and-georgia-1780-82/. Accessed May 12, 2022; Robert Stansbury Lambert, *South Carolina Loyalists in the American Revolution* (Columbia: University of South Carolina Press, 1987), 104–5.
13. See Cornwallis to Balfour, August 29, 1780, Saberton, *CP*, Vol. II, 64. They were to be employed to protect the region between Camden and Charleston.
14. Balfour to Cornwallis, October 26, 1780, Saberton, *CP*, Vol. II, 132.
15. Colonel Robert Gray to Lord Cornwallis, November 5, 1780; the letter was addressed as "Post at Colonel Thomson's," implying a fort rather than a camp, Saberton, *CP*, Vol. III, 394.
16. Salley, *History*, 378.
17. Ibid., 381.
18. See, for instance, John Cruden's letter to "Bean," May 31, 1782, Saberton, *CP*, Vol VI, 290–91, in which he lists all the areas where the British had taken "support" from sequestered estates; "Motts House" is included.
19. Balfour to Rawdon, November 1, 1780, Saberton, *CP*, Vol. III, 61.
20. This may have been Loyalist John Coffin, who would be promoted to major during the war and take part in the Battle of Hobkirk's Hill. He would retire to Canada after the war and raise a regiment in the War of 1812, eventually becoming a major general. Saberton, *CP*, Vol. II, 94; George Turnbull to Lord Cornwallis, November 3, 1780, Saberton, *CP*, Vol. III, 136.

21. Balfour to Cornwallis, December 11, 1780, Saberton, *CP*, Vol. III, 111.
22. Balfour to Cornwallis, December 26, 1780, Saberton, *CP*, Vol. III, 116.
23. Cornwallis to Rawdon, December 17, 1780, Saberton, *CP*, Vol. III, 216.
24. Rawdon to Cornwallis, December 25, 1780, Saberton, *CP*, Vol. III, 226.
25. Balfour to Cornwallis, December 16, 1780, Saberton, *CP*, Vol. III, 114; Balfour to Cornwallis, June 14, 1780, in Saberton, *CP*, Vol. I, 90.
26. James, 91; Marion to Greene, January 31, 1781, *GP*, Vol. VII, 229; David Ramsay, *History of the Revolution of South Carolina From a British Province To An Independent State* (Trenton [NJ?]: Isaac Collins, 1785), 209. James has the officer's efforts reversed, with Colonel, not Captain, John Postell at Manigault's.
27. Saberton, note, *CP*, Vol IV, 29, 181. Marion and Sumter biographer Robert Bass states that Charles McPherson commanded at Belleville. Although Bass's citation methods are not precise, he is often right. It's very possible Charles McPherson was at Belleville, in charge of troops but not post commander. Robert Bass, *Gamecock: The Life and Campaigns of General Thomas Sumter* (Orangeburg, SC: Sandlapper Publishing, Inc., 2000, original 1961), 130. McPherson would be the post commander at Fort Motte.
28. Lieutenant Colonel Nisbet Balfour wrote that he thought Sumter had seven hundred or eight hundred men; Balfour to Clinton, February 24, 1781, Clinton Papers.
29. McCrady, 107–8; Salley, *History*, 379.
30. C. Leon Harris and Charles B. Baxley, "To Keep Up the Spirits of the People and Alarm the Enemy: Sumter's Rounds in South Carolina, February 16–March 9, 1781," *Southern Campaigns of the American Revolution*, 20, no. 3 (2022): 16–17. Harris and Baxley state that Sumter was at Manigault's plantation.
31. McCrady, 108. Like many battles, casualty and captured goods figures are inconsistent. Harris and Baxley list pension applications that state the number of wagons ranged from seven to eighteen. Greene wrote that the British lost sixty men. Greene to Huntington, March 23, 1781; *GP*, Vol. VII, 465.
32. Harris and Baxley, *Southern Campaigns*, 19.
33. Ibid.
34. Lipscomb, *Names In South Carolina*, Vol. XXIV, 16–17; Lipscomb, *Revolutionary Battles.*
35. Thomas Sumter to Greene, January 13, 1781, *GP*, Vol. VII, 118.
36. Balfour to Lieutenant McPherson, January 21, 1781; Joseph W. Barnwell, "Letters to General Greene and Others," *SCHGM* XVII, no. 1 (1916), 3.
37. Lee, *Memoirs*, 345.
38. Rebecca E. Shepherd, "Going Up Country: A Comparison of Elite Ceramic Consumption Patterns in Charleston and the Carolina Frontier" (Master's Thesis, Department of Anthropology, University of South Carolina, 2014), 63–68.
39. SCIAA archaeologist James B. Legg is acknowledged for making this observation.
40. Rankin, *Francis Marion*, The *Swamp Fox* (New York: Thomas Crowell Company, 1973), 201. Rankin mistakenly calls the plantation "Mount Pleasant."
41. Francis Rawdon to Henry Lee, June 24, 1813, in Lee, *Memoirs*, 615.
42. Sumter to Greene, April 7, 1781, *GP*, Vol. VIII, 67.

43. This is asserted by Anne King Gregorie, 138.
44 Balfour to Cornwallis, April 20, 1781, Saberton, *CP*, Vol IV, 172.
45. Major Andrew Maxwell was commander at Fort Granby on the "Congarees."
46. Sumter to Greene, May 2, 1781, *GP*, Vol. VIII, 193. A well appeared in October 2015 after a one-in-a-thousand-year weather event occurred over an eleven-day period of continual rain in South Carolina. The author cannot confirm it was the same well, however the well was just outside the fort as Sumter noted, adjacent to the fort ditch. When Benson Lossing visited Fort Motte in the late 1840s, he claimed the same well was still in use; Lossing, 477. Lossing also noted that a depression was evident where the soldiers had built a covered way to protect them when getting water. If so, they were in a direct line of fire from the Americans' 6-pounder cannon.
47. In keeping with the strange circumstances surrounding the abandonment of Belleville and occupation of Mount Joseph is an intriguing and baffling letter written by Captain James Conyers to General Nathanael Greene, April 14, 1781, *GP*, Vol. VIII, 95. Conyers was an aide to Greene involved in gathering cattle and horses for the army. In the letter, Conyers wrote from "Col Thomsons" that he "waited" on Thomson and found that the militia "have taken Col Thomsons horses, which I shall seize as soon as I get to Gen Marion," obviously implicating Marion's militia. Furthermore, he asked Thomson to "assist in procuring horses" and Conyers notes that no man will be more serviceable. Thomson asked for a special order to impress horses and forage. Most amazing, Conyers indicates that Thomson's plantation "is as safe from any inroads of Plundering Rascals as any in the country good pasturage and neighborhood where forage may be had." He also requests two dragoons to assist in the feeding of horses until they are forwarded to Greene.

Thus, only a few days after Belleville is abandoned by the British, Thomson was assisting Greene in the gathering of horses needed to mount Greene's dragoons, and Conyers thought Belleville was safe from plunderers. The editors of the Greene Papers state that Thomson had another plantation on Thomson's Creek in the upcountry of South Carolina; *GP*, Vol VIII, 95 n.1. Thomson's Creek drains into the Pee Dee in modern Chesterfield County. However, there is no record of a William Thomson having any property on Thomson's Creek in the state archives deed book or plat books (the creek appears to have been named for an early eighteenth-century Thomson, not Colonel William). No local historians have found any connection between Colonel William Thomson of Orangeburg District and the Thomsons in that region. The papers of the William Thomson family do not indicate or mention any property in that area. See Papers of William Thomson, South Caroliniana Library, University of South Carolina, Columbia. The only explanation is that this letter concerns Colonel Thomson of Belleville Plantation, who was indeed at home at Belleville at that time.

CHAPTER FIVE: THE SIEGE AND CAPTURE OF FORT MOTTE

1. The diaries of Evan Pugh, along the Pee Dee, and Samuel Mathis, near Camden, note that the day was cold and wet, Mathis stating "Rain very hard all day." Indeed, throughout the siege, it was cold, with frost on the ninth and tenth. See Pugh, 206; Samuel Mathis Papers, March–July 1781, South Caroliniana Library, University of South Carolina. An archaeological profile of the fort's ditch reveals a bottom level of wall slump probably as a result of the rain.

2. Marion to Greene, May 6, 1781, *GP*, Vol. VIII, 214. Although he stated he had only 150 men, they were from quite an assortment of units, including six companies of the Berkeley County Regiment, four companies of Horry's Light Dragoons, three companies of the Nash County North Carolina militia, one company of Warren County North Carolina militia, and some Virginia volunteers from Nottoway County. J. D. Lewis, "The Evolution of Marion's Brigade After the Fall of Charleston 1780 to 1782," slide presentation, www.carolana.com. Although Lewis lists all these units, it's probable they were nowhere near full strength and this list only represents the variety of units.

3. Robert Wright states that it was a partisan corps, but Greene and Lee refer to it as a legion. Robert K. Wright, Jr., *The Continental Army* (Washington, DC: Center of Military History, United States Army, 1983), 161. J. D. Lewis lists three hundred men of six troops. Lewis, *Evolution.*

4. Rankin, *The North Carolina Continentals*, 329–31. These may have numbered as many as 115 men. There were probably three companies. Lewis, *Evolution.*

5. The strength total here is from the prisoner returns documented in the *Papers of the Continental Congress*, M247, R175, I 155, Vol. 2: 8. Some secondary sources point out that there were 165 men captured, and they are correct, according to the prisoner returns of soldiers. However, there were in addition to the privates, a captain, three lieutenants, three ensigns, a sergeant major and a sergeant, eight corporals, and two drummers or fifers, totaling 184. Both Greene and Rawdon report that 140 men were captured at Fort Motte in various correspondence, but Greene's Orderly Book reports "Seven commissioned officers, and one-hundred and seventy-three noncommissioned officers and privates." William Lamar, Nathanael Greene's Orderly Book, Fergusson Collection, on file, Society of The Cincinnati, Washington, DC.

6. The 84th were Scottish soldiers known as the Royal Highland Emigrants mostly from Canada and wore kilts like the Black Watch. https://www.84th-rhe.com/1780, accessed January 19, 2023; Lewis, *Evolution.* Garrison Orders, May 30, Charleston, *Royal Gazette*, Vol. 1, No. 26, names Captain Neil Campbell as commander of the troops at Motte's house.

7. Starcloff's Hessians Troop of Light Dragoons was formed near Charleston in April of 1781 composed of men from Hesse-Cassel. They probably were disbanded when Charleston was abandoned in December 1782. Dornfest, *Loyalists*, 399; Philip R. N. Katcher, *Encyclopedia of British, Provincial, and German Army Units, 1775–1783* (Harrisburg, PA: Stackpole Books, 1973), 101.

8. Balfour to Cornwallis, May 21, 1781, Saberton, *CP*, Vol. V, 276.

9. Sumter reported that two cannon had been delivered Saturday, May 5, by a "party of horse." Sumter to Greene, May 7, 1781, *GP*, Vol. III, 221.

10. Levi Smith, states that "Captain" McPherson, post commander, was with Delancy's Corps. Smith was correct about McPherson's unit. Sometimes McPherson's rank is listed as lieutenant, including Charleston Garrison Orders of May 29, 1781, in the *Royal Gazette*, and Lord Rawdon's letter of condolences to the lieutenant, written May 14, and published in the *Royal Gazette*, June 6, 1781. In the list of army officers, he is listed as "Captain Lieutenant" Charles McPherson in DeLancy's Corps listed in 1783. See *List of Officers of the Army* (London: War Office, 1783, 87), [hereinafter] *LOO*]. Some historians, including Hugh F. Rankin, state McPherson's first name was Donald. Rankin, *Swamp Fox*, 201. There was a Lieutenant Donald McPherson with the 1st Battalion of the 71st in 1781 (*LOO* 1781, 145; *LOO* 1783, 40), and a Captain Donald McPherson in the British Legion (*LOO* 1783, 79). Confirming that the Fort Motte commander was Charles McPherson is a letter written on May 5, 1781, from Charles McPherson to Major Maxwell, which is posted from Mottes, "Chas McPherson to Major Maxwell," May 5, 1781, Auction Lot 6, Fall Historical Auction Sale, Alexander Historical Auctions, Stamford, CT, October 9, 2010, copy in author's possession.

Charles McPherson was born in Scotland in 1755 and was captured at sea in April of 1779. He was exchanged sometime between October 1780 and January 1781, only to be captured again at Fort Motte four months later. After the war, he stayed in the military and was eventually promoted to major and inspector general of barracks in Scotland in 1812. During the Southern Campaign he was a respected officer who was, like McKay, lauded for his defense of his post. He died in Edinburgh in 1820. Dornfest, *Loyalists*, 241. The fact that he was an inspector general of barracks suggests he was a trained engineer or assistant engineer, which would account for the well-designed and constructed Fort Motte. Charles Brian Mabelitini, "British Fortification Strategy in the South Carolina Backcountry During the Southern Campaign of the American Revolution: Archaeological and Historical Perspectives on Infrastructure and Landscape" (PhD diss., University of South Carolina, 2024), 53–54.

11. As far as the others, Smith asserts that all those listed herein were "eyewitnesses" to his adventure and thus at Fort Motte at the time of the siege. Besides Captain Neil Campbell (LOO 1783, 48), there was Lieutenants Robert Amiel (LOO 1783, 24), Walter Partridge (LOO 1781, 93, LOO 1782, 93), John Hildebrand (LOO 1783, 63), and Henry Lory [Lorey] (LOO 1783, 55).

12. Marion to Greene, May 12, 1781, in *GP*, Vol. VIII, 246.

13. Engineer's drawing of Fort Motte, E. M. Hyrne, Papers of the Continental Congress, Record Group 360, M247: 89; Smith et al., 2007.

14. The engineering plan of the fort indicates the wall began some ten feet from the house, while the profile makes it appear to be only two or three feet from the house.

15. The engineer's drawing appears to show a square fort; however, an AutoCAD analysis completed by Jonna Wallace Mabelitini indicates that its actually 115 by 125 feet. This is remarkably close to what the archaeological excavations indicated. See Mabelitini, "British Fortification Strategy," 509.

16. The exact size was 98 x 121 feet inside. It can be assumed the British engineer intended 100 x 120.

17. The profile, however, was not exactly perpendicular to the ditch, about 10 degrees offset, making the actual width narrower,

18. A Fort Motte mystery is where the British regulars, like the 84th Foot and Hessians, camped prior to the beginning of the siege. Intensive and systematic metal detecting in the field surrounding the fort has failed to find any concentration of unfired .75-caliber musket balls that fit the standard land pattern musket of the British regulars, (often called the "Brown Bess" in the early nineteenth century), which would suggest a British campground. There is a scatter of buckshot and musket balls about 260 yards south. The musket balls were the kind of balls that would have been fired from French Charleville muskets (i.e., .69-caliber), suggesting either an American Continental camp or a Loyalist camp. Another 200 yards south of that site a frizzen from German musket was found, suggesting the Hessian presence at Fort Motte, but no other indications of a camp. Some 360 yards southwest of the fort is still another concentration of buckshot and .69-caliber musket balls. There are a few unfired .75-caliber musket balls in and around the fort interior as would be expected, likely to have been lost during the siege. While relic collectors certainly have affected archaeological interpretations, work by the South Carolina Institute of Archaeology and Anthropology has been conducted in ideal metal detecting conditions of plowed fields, while the relic collectors were operating in a forest environment with heavy undergrowth. The lack of a dense collection of unfired musket balls except at the fort, only reinforces the conclusion that the fort had only been in existence for a few weeks prior to the siege and the British had very recently arrived.

19. Sumter to Greene, May 2, 1781, *GP*, Vol. VIII, 193. It must be admitted that this well also could have been dug during the early nineteenth-century occupation of Mount Joseph.

20. Lossing, *Field Book*, 148. There are two narrow parallel lines on the engineer's drawing of the fort, which may be the engineer's depiction of a covered way.

21. Levi Smith, "To the Printers," *Royal Gazette*, April 17, 1782.

22. The cluster of unfired buckshot was recovered by 130 yards east of the fort running north-south with a gap of no lead shot between. This suggests the presence of an open forest at the time of the siege, from which Marion's riflemen could emerge, fire at the fort, and retreat to safety.

23. Lee, *Memoirs*, 345.

24. Smith, *Royal Gazette*.

25. Alexander Garden states that the Mottes had been allowed to stay in an "apartment" until Belleville was "carried," when McPherson thought it best for them to be removed. Belleville, however, was not carried but abandoned by the British. "Mrs. Brewton," in Alexander Garden, *Anecdotes of the Revolutionary War in America: With Sketches of Character of Persons the Most Distinguished, In the Southern States, For Civil and Military Service* (Charleston, SC: A. E. Miller, 1822), 231. Archaeologists found a chatelaine just upslope of the base of the hill where the old farmhouse was located. As chatelaines were traditionally the mark of a wealthy housekeeper or madame of the manor, it is reasonable to assume it was either Rebecca Motte's, or Mrs. Lloyd's, who the author believes was living in

the house many years before Rebecca owned the property, or perhaps it was the overseer's wife. Rebecca is the most likely owner.

26. Lee, *Memoirs,* 346–47.

27. Little is known about these enslaved people and their fate. Twenty of the slaves came from William Bull's plantation about two miles away. Bull, formerly lieutenant governor of South Carolina and a Loyalist, had a total of 180 at his Congaree plantation, and the remaining 160 would be confiscated by Thomas Sumter later, to be distributed to his militia as part of "Sumter's Law." Many of the enslaved on Bull's plantation had been brought from a plantation on St. Helena's Island for safety in 1779. It is also reasonable to assume some had built the fort when the British occupied Mount Joseph. Kinloch Bull Jr., *The Oligarchs in Colonial and Revolutionary Charleston: Lieutenant Governor William Bull II and His Family* (Columbia: University of South Carolina Press, 1991), 290; Lee, *Memoirs,* 345.

28. The entrance to the sap has not been precisely located; however a depression approximately thirty yards north from the northern end of the sap as seen on the GRP map (Figure 11) strongly suggests its location. No excavations have been completed there to confirm.

29. Lee, *Memoirs,* 345.

30. In the 1980s, during a logging episode, the mound was accidentally pushed back into the hole the slaves dug to get the soil to build it, however, it can be seen in a 1930s aerial photo. In 2014, archaeologists located the remains of the mound and recovered a 6-pound iron cannon ball.

31. Stacey R. Whitacre, "An Analysis of Lead Shot From Fort Motte, 2004–2012: Assessing Combat Behavior in Terms of Agency" (master's thesis, University of South Carolina, 2013), 118.

32. Lee specifically states that the British were "unprovided with artillery," however, archaeological investigations recovered iron canister along the sap all the way to its entrance and downhill. These shots could not have been fired by the American artillery. Lee, *Memoirs,* 345.

33. An interesting, but unexplained aspect of the rife balls recovered from Fort Motte is that they are primarily of the fifteen-gram weight, which corresponds to .54-caliber. The distribution of lead shot from Fort Watson, merely two weeks prior, and logically the same rifle detachment, indicates a wide distribution in rifle ball weights, which would be expected. This suggests that while there were numerous riflemen firing at Fort Watson, perhaps only two riflemen (both rifled and smooth bore rifle shot was found of this weight, indicating two different rifles) were the primary sharpshooters firing at the British at Fort Motte. Admittedly stretching the data, perhaps the two sharpshooters were Lieutenant Allen McDonald and a Lieutenant Cruger (Cryer), both casualties of the siege. McDonald was a known sharpshooter famous for his exploits, while Cruger "emulated" McDonald. McDonald, however, was killed at the beginning of the siege. See James, 121; Whitacre, 132–33.

34. Sumter to Greene, May 6 and 7, 1781, *GP,* Vol. VIII, 218, 221.

35. Gregorie, 157–58; *GP,* notes Vol. VIII, 244. Several pension applications mention Sumter's men being at Fort Motte briefly; see George Gill S21229, James

Veale W9586, Thomas Young S10309, James Clinton S2437. Some may have been confused with Belleville though. Interestingly, they do not mention assisting Marion; instead they say they were assisting the Continentals.
36. Thomas Young Pension S10309. See also, Daniel Carter S3126, Ralph Rodgers S4788, Samuel Otterson S25344, William Polk S3706, William Hutchison W10133. Many of these men started at Fort Motte, and then went with Sumter to Orangeburg.
37. Ervin to Greene, May 6, 1781, *GP*, Vol. VIII, 213.
38. Greene to Thomas Jefferson, April 6, 1780, *GP*, VIII, 58.
39. Greene to Marion, January 16, 1781, and Marion to Greene, January 20, 1781, in *GP*, Vol. VII, 131, 165.
40. Greene to Marion, April 27, 1781, in *GP*, Vol. VIII, 160–61.
41. Lee and Sumter to Greene, May 2, 1781, *GP*, Vol. VIII, 192–94. Note, Lee states that Marion has 150 horses, the exact number of troops Marion has at the time.
42. Marion to Greene, May 6, *GP*, Vol. VIII, 214–15.
43. Greene to Marion, May 9, *GP*, Vol. VIII, 230-231.
44. Marion to Sumter, both May 10, 1781, Thomas Sumter Papers, William Draper Collection, Microfilm copies, South Carolina Department of Archives and History, Columbia, SC.
45. Marion to Greene, *GP*, Vol. VIII, 243.
46. Marion to Greene, *GP*, Vol. VII, 207. Interestingly, Lee does not mention Marion in his dispatches to Greene about the attack on Georgetown.
47. Lee to Greene, April 20, 1781, *GP*, Vol. VIII, 125; Lee to Greene, April 23, 1781, *GP*, Vol. VIII, 139.
48. Lee to Greene, May 8, 1781, *GP*, Vol. VIII, 223. Lee doesn't think much of Sumter either.
49. Greene to Lee, May 9, 1781, *GP*, Vol. VIII, 228.
50. Lee, *Memoirs*, 585.
51. William Davie, Recollection, *GP*, Vol. VIII, 225.
52. Terry Golway, *Washington's General: Nathanael Greene and the Triumph of the American Revolution* (New York: John Macrae Book, Henry Holt and Company, 2005), 270.
53. Rawdon to Cornwallis, May 24, 1781, Saberton, *CP*, Vol. V, 289.
54. Excavation of a portion of the sap indicated that it averaged thirty inches wide (Figure 20). It's impossible to know how deep it was, but from the modern plowed surface it was at least 3.5 feet deep, so maybe 4 feet at the time it was dug. Although the walls were rather ragged, the excavations suggest the diggers took some care in the floor of the trench, making it flat with rounded corners.
55. Marion to Greene, May 11, 1781, *GP*, Vol. VIII, 242.
56. Lee, *Memoirs*, 346. Some historians dispute that Rawdon's campfires could be seen from Mount Joseph. Whether they could or not, Marion was aware of Rawdon's march south past the high hills of the Santee and that the British at Nelson's Ferry were gathering boats for the crossing. See Marion to Greene, May 12, 1781, *GP*, Vol. VIII, 246.
57. Lee, *Memoirs*, 347.
58. Ibid., 347.

59. Ibid., 347. Lee states that he spoke to Mrs. Motte. Other versions have Marion or both speaking to Mrs. Motte.
60. C. C. Pinckney, letter to the Columbia *Carolinian*, Flat Rock, September 27, 1855, quoted in Salley, "Miles Brewton," 149.
61. Letter of Harriet P. Rutledge, October 9, 1855, attached to Letter of C. C. Pinckney. Pinckney Family Papers, South Carolina Historical Society, Charleston, SC (43/1096).
62. Garden, 231.
63. Ibid., 232. According to Garden, after the surrender Polly Brewton taunted a British ensign named Amiel who had previously provoked the women by boasting to them of his "prowess" by cutting saplings with his sword while naming them Greene, Marion, Sumter, etc. Seeing him defeated, she quipped: "Is Marion no more to feel the power of your arm, nor Sumter be compelled to bite the dust?" Among the author's favorite Brewton lines was her reply to a British officer when she arrived in Charleston after the siege, who asked her what news there was in the upcountry, to which she replied, "all nature smiled, for everything was *Greene* down to Monk's Corner." A supposed veteran of the siege puts these words into the mouth of Mrs. Motte. Benson Lossing, *Reflections of Rebellion Hours With the Living Men and Women of the Revolution* (Charleston, SC: The History Press, 2005, original 1889), 51; but see n.246.
64. Several other sources, possibly referring to Pinckney's letter, state that a musket or rifle was used. See for instance, Mrs. O. J. Weslin and Miss Anges Irvin, *Worthy Women of Our First Century* (Philadelphia: J.B. Lippenwith Co., 1877), 271; "Tablet to Mrs. Rebecca Motte," Program, D.A.R. Ceremony of Unveiling at St. Philips Church, Charleston, South Carolina, May 9, 1903 (Daggett Printing Company, 1903), on file, South Caroliniana Library.
65. See Cote, n.16.
66. Roderick Mackenzie, *Strictures of Lt. Col. Tarleton's History of the Campaigns of 1780 and 1781* (London, 1787), 151–52.
67. James suffered from smallpox when Marion was fighting Watson in March 1781. He is unclear exactly when he took the field with Marion and became an eyewitness to Marion's exploits.
68. James, *Sketch*, 120–21, and Simms, 238. Benson Lossing visited Mount Joseph in 1849 and met an unidentified veteran of the siege. The veteran also names Nathan Savage as the soldier who fired the arrows. In the veteran's version, someone made a bow and arrows and took them to the overseer's house where Savage and Lee were. Savage said the bow was not strong enough and that is when Rebecca offered her bow. The veteran's story of the siege is amazingly detailed for a ninety-three-year-old (says he was twenty-five in 1781) and gives the author pause as to its full veracity. His account reads as if he had read the story in some book, probably James. Benson Lossing, *Reflections*, 47–51. Nathan Savage lived northwest of Snow's Island, across Lynches Creek and was a stalwart member of Marion's Brigade. See Smith, *Francis Marion*, 77.
69. These measurements are based on the engineering drawing of the fort (see Figure 10). The abatis would have kept Savage from approaching within thirty feet of the fort ditch.

70. And it does work. Archaeologist James Legg and former USC undergraduate student Ellan Hambright prepared their own arrows and Legg fired them from his replica Charleville flintlock musket. Steven D. Smith, Brian Mabelitini, James B. Legg, and Ellan Hambright, "Two Revolutionary War Expedient Fire Arrows From Archaeological Contexts in South Carolina, *Journal of the Company of Military Historians*, 71, no. 3: 243–46. Ellan Hambright, senior thesis, University of South Carolina, 2016.
71. The fire arrow was found with a concentration of .69 caliber musket balls downhill from the sap entrance. This most likely was a work area for Continental soldiers overseeing the excavation of the sap.
72. Harrison, 41.
73. Letter, Rawdon to Cornwallis, May 24, 1781, in Walter Clark, ed., *The State Records of North Carolina, Volume XVII, 1781–85* (Goldsboro, NC: Nash Bro. Book and Job Printers, 1899), 1031–35. Besides Lee, *Memoir* and James, and Lord Rawdon's letter, see a 1788 history of the United States, which also indicates that the house was set afire by fire arrows. It was written only a few years after the war, and before any of the more mythological biographies of Marion by Weems and William Gilmore Simms were written. See William Gordon, *The History Rise, Progress, and Establishment of the United States of America*, Four Volumes, (London, 1788), 89–90; Simms, 238; Horry and Weems, 220.
74. Lee, *Memoirs*, 348.
75. A. S. Salley, *History*, 379; Rawdon to Cornwallis, May 24, 181, in Saberton, *CP*, Vol. V, 289.

CHAPTER SIX: AFTER THE SIEGE

1. See endnote 45, chapter one, for more on McDonald.
2. James names him Cryer, 121. William Gilmore Simms calls him Cruger, Simms, 238.
3. Orderly Book, Lieutenant Hector MacClean, 84th Infantry, William Clements Library, University of Michigan, Ann Arbor, MI. Correspondence with Todd Braisted, July 23, 2013, and Kim Stacy, October 24, 2023.
4. Captain Frederick Starcloff's Light Dragoons' muster rolls lists Corporal John Ludwick (or Ludwick, John), privates Daniel Klamberg, Johannes Peter, Jacob Muller, Johannes Caliproh, Johannes Hick, Jacob Eydam, Johan Jost Horn, Jacob Busch, Joel Rensenier, Philip Herge, Johannes Kochler, Johannes Lapp, and Mingus Schloux as captured on May 12. Muster roll for CPT Starcloff's Light Dragoons, Burgoyne Collection, Box 1, Folder 2, National Society of the Sons of the American Revolution, Louisville, Kentucky.
5. *Papers of the Continental Congress*, M247, Item 155, Vol. 2, 83. May 16, 1781.
6. Letter, Greene to Samuel Huntington, May 14, 1781, *GP*, Vol. VIII, 250–53. Interestingly, this letter, with slightly different wording appears in Tarleton's *History of the Southern Campaigns* and in Gibbes, *Documentary History*. For instance, the captured materials are listed as "one carronade, one hundred and forty muskets, a quantity of salt provisions, and other stores." Gibbes, *Documentary History Vol. I*, 71. Lieutenant Colonel Banastre Tarleton, *A History of the Campaigns of*

1780 and 1781 in the Southern Provinces of North America (Cranbury NJ: The Scholar's Bookshelf, 2005, original 1787), 475

7. However, it may be the exact opposite; see below. The Loyalists were dragged north with Lee, while the regulars were paroled downstream to Nelson's Ferry.

8. Lee, *Memoirs*, 348.

9. Simms, 238–39. Simms took this story from Horry and Weems's biography of Francis Marion so it may be completely fanciful. Weems's book, based on Peter Horry's manuscript, is an amazing mixture of fact and fantasy. As Weems tells the tale of the siege of Fort Motte, he states that the siege was a "sharp contest, in which many valuable lives were lost on both sides" and Mrs. Motte, upon hearing that her house must burn, exclaimed "O! burn it! burn it, general Marion! God forbid I should bestow a single thought on my little concerns, when the independence of my country is at stake—No sir, if it were a palace it should go." At the same time, he notes that the arrows were pointed with iron (correct as the archaeological evidence proves), and as we will see, names Levi Smith and Hugh Mizcally as victims of vigilante justice. See below. Horry and Weems, 222–23.

10. Edward McCrady states that the British officers were paroled and sent to Rawdon the evening of the surrender. See McCrady, 235. Likewise does Lee, *Memoirs*, 349. Levi Smith says it was the next morning as does Weems.

11. Smith, *Royal Gazette*, April 17, 1782. Smith's story is certainly self-promoting, but it adds interesting details about the conduct of the siege.

12. How Smith knew why Fulker was killed is not clear, as he was in the millhouse at the time. The British did not forget Lieutenant Fulker's hanging. American militia lieutenant colonel Isaac Hayne was captured by the British in July 1781. He had previously been captured at the fall of Charleston in May 1780, taken a parole, and returned to his Colleton County plantation. The British soon demanded that paroled militia take an oath of allegiance, and Hayne complied, but when they then demanded he take up arms against the Americans, he considered it a breach of his parole. He rejoined the American forces where he was once again captured. Hayne was hanged on August 4, 1781.

This set off a series of bitter correspondence between the British and Americans about the treatment of prisoners, and Fulker's hanging was among those the British brought up as examples of American treatment of captured British officers. Colonel Nisbet Balfour wrote Greene, "Sir, it will not be Unapposite, to remark, that at the very Period when Lieut. [T]ulcer of the Loyal Militia was publicky executed at Mott's house, Numbers of your Officers were absolutely in my power, . . . without efforts to secure them, by the hands of Licensed & Protected Murderers." After countering Balfour's other arguments, Greene takes note of the fate of Fulker, stating, "The execution of Lieu Tulker was without my knowledge or consent, nor did I ever hear of it before. I understood there were some, who fell a sacrifice to the violence of the militia, for the many outrages they had been guilty of, and this without the knowledge of the commanding Officer, who put a stop to it the moment he discovered it. But there is a great difference between deliberate executions, & deaths which happen from an enraged people urged by a sense of injury & oppression." Thus, Greene quibbles a bit. He obviously knew about the hangings and that Marion stopped them;

he just didn't know the victims' names. Balfour to Greene, September 3, 1781, *GP*, Vol. IX, 284; Greene to Balfour, September 19, 1781, *GP*. Vol. IX, 372.

13. For some reason, although the Loyalists supposedly surrendered to the militia, the Continentals were involved in the hangings. It's possible that the militia were guarding the millhouse and thus were complicit in allowing the Continentals to take them.

14. Again, how did Smith know these details about Miscally [aka Maskelly, Mizcally]? Miscally had property on Muddy Creek, adjacent to Snow's Island and was named as a guide to British colonel Doyle, who had raided Marion's camp on Snow's in March 1781. It's reasonable to assume he showed them where Marion was camped. It should be mentioned, however, that Smith indicates Miscally guided Doyle to Camden in April, after the camp was raided, yet the coincidence is rather remarkable and perhaps he had guided Doyle earlier also. Incidentally, records in the South Carolina archives indicate that Miscally's wife remained on Muddy Creek for several years after the war before moving to a property north of Snow's Island. Thus, she was not harassed, nor did she lose her land for her husband's loyalism. Smith, *Francis Marion*, 158–59.

15. Smith, *Royal Gazette*, April 17, 1782. Like the meal at Mrs. Motte's, exactly when this event took place is not clear. Weems states that during the meal with the British officers at Mrs. Motte's house, the feast was interrupted by a British soldier who arrived and whispered in the ear of an officer, who in turn told Marion that they were hanging the Loyalists. Marion immediately set out to stop them. Lee makes no mention of hanging any Loyalists. Smith, the surviving victim, says it occurred the next morning, which if true, suggests the Weems version is apocryphal. For the record, our old veteran interviewed by Benson Lossing in the 1840s states that it was a Tom Cunningham whom Marion saved from hanging. Cunningham is not mentioned in any other version of the story. Lossing, *Reflections*, 51.

16. Smith left South Carolina and settled in East Florida after the war. He claimed 850 acres, twenty-one slaves, and a store before the war, and received 1,358 pounds sterling for his loss. See Gregory Palmer, *Biographical Sketches of Loyalists of the American Revolution* (Westport, CT: Meckler Publishing, 1984), 802.

17. Lee, *Memoirs*, 348.

18. Joseph Johnson, *Traditions and Reminiscences Chiefly of the American Revolution* (Spartanburg, SC: The Reprint Company, 1972, original 1851), 101.

19. See Lee, *Memoirs*, Letter from Lord Rawdon, 615–16. See also, Lord Rawdon to Lord Cornwallis, May 24, 1781, in Walter Clark, ed., *Records of North Carolina*, 1031–35; Nelson, *Francis-Lord Rawdon Hastings*, 95–98.

20. Letter from Rawdon, 615. Rawdon's letter explains many of the puzzling decisions he made throughout that spring of 1781. Rawdon operated under the understanding that he had no responsibility for the region of the Santee, Congaree, and Saluda Rivers, which was Balfour's problem. Furthermore, Balfour as a lieutenant colonel "of the line" therefore out-ranked Rawdon and was his superior. Rawdon had been given a promotion by Clinton, but it did not arrive until Rawdon left South Carolina after the siege of Fort Motte. During that en-

tire spring and summer, Rawdon and Balfour acted upon the idea that Balfour was his superior, and that Rawdon's main concern was holding Camden and "the frontiers beyond the rivers." See Letter from Rawdon, 615–16.
21. Letter, Rawdon to Cornwallis, May 24, 1781, *State Records*, 1031–35.
22. Rawdon to Cornwallis, May 24, 1781, Saberton, *CP*, Vol. V, 289.
23. Letter, Rawdon to Cornwallis, May 24, 1781, *State Records*, 1031–35
24. Letter, Rawdon to Lee, May 14, 1781, in Gibbes, *Documentary History, Vol. I*, 70.
25. It is interesting to note that Greene states in his letter to Samuel Huntington that 140 men were captured, 120 of which were British and Hessian, with seven or eight officers. Letter, Greene to Huntington, May 14, 1781, *GP*, Volume VIII, 251. This is inconsistent with the inventory in the Papers of the Continental Congress, even if he left out the 45 Loyalists. When it comes to killed, wounded, captured, and missing battle casualties, this is hardly unique or even unusual.
26. General Orders, Head Quarters, New Windsor, June 15, 1781, in John C. Fitzpatrick, ed., *The Writings of George Washington, Volume 22, April 27, 1781–August 15, 1781* (Washington, DC: United States Printing Office, 1931), 215–16. This number is consistent with the Papers of the Continental Congress.
27. Lee, *Memoirs*, 345; Letter, Greene to Samuel Huntington, May 14, 1781, *GP*, Vol. VIII, 251.
28. Lee, *Memoirs*, 348.
29. Letter from Rawdon to McPherson, *Royal Gazette*, June 6, 1781.
30. Rawdon to Cornwallis, May 24, 1781, in Saberton, *CP*, Vol. V, 289.
31. Garrison Orders, May 29, 1781, in *Royal Gazette*, May 30, 1781.
32. Clinton to Rawdon, July 13, 1781, *Clinton Papers*, Vol. 164, folder 22.
33. Sumter to Greene, May 15, 16, 22, 1781, *GP*, Vol. VIII, 269, 274, 297; Greene to Sumter, May 17, 1781, *GP*, Vol. VIII, 277–78.
34. James, 121; Lossing, *Field Book*, 148.
35. Letter, Pendleton to Simmons, November 9, 1781, *GP*, Vol. IX, 551.
36. Lieut. William Feltman, *The Journal of Lieut. William Feltman, of the First Pennsylvania Regiment, 1781–1782* (Philadelphia, PA: Henry Carey Baird for the Historical Society of Pennsylvania, 1853), 32–33; Bobby Gilmore Moss, *Roster of South Carolina Patriots in the American Revolution* (Baltimore, MD: Genealogical Publishing Co., 1983), 232; Margaret F. Pickett, pers. comm., May 18, 2023.
37. Pinckney to Greene, *GP*, Vol. X, 566–67; Pickett, 123–25.
38. Lee to Greene, August 8, 1781, and Letter, Doctor Robert Johnson to Greene, *GP*, Vol. IX, 150, 274. See also letter of a Col. Williams to Major Giles, September 23, 1781, in, N.C. Brooks, "Battle of Eutaw Springs," *Graham's Magazine*, Volume XVII, December 1845, 256–57.
39. There are some references to the army being camped at McCord's Ferry; however, Greene's Orderly Book states "Camp at Fort Motte, September 2–4, 1781." The Orderly Book of General Nathanael Greene, Society of the Cincinnati, Washington, DC. Figure 13 depicts two concentrations of lead shot to the south of Fort Motte. These concentrations consisted overwhelmingly of buckshot and .69-caliber musket balls, suggesting either American Continental camps after the siege or Loyalist camps prior to the siege. The former is more likely.

40. Greene to Thomas McKean, September 11, 1781, *GP*, Vol. IX, 328.
41. Greene to Linton, March 14, 1783, *GP*, Vol. XII, 512–13.
42. Major Ichabod Burnet to Greene, *GP*, Vol. X, 529–30. Burnet was escorting Mrs. Greene.
43. Captain John Joyner to Greene, *GP*, Vol. XI, 629.
44. Pickett, 158, 160–61. Rebecca Motte died on January 10, 1815. Thomas Pinckney was elected governor of South Carolina in 1787 and U.S. minister to Great Britain in 1792. Gregory D. Massey, "Thomas Pinckney," in *South Carolina Encyclopedia*, ed. Walter Edgar (Columbia: University of South Carolina Press, 2006), 731–32.

EPILOGUE

1. Balfour to Germain, June 27, 1781, K. G. Davies, *Documents of the American Revolution 1770–1783*, Volume XX, Transcripts 1781 (Dublin: Irish University Press, 1979), 163. The mention that the prisoners were less than six hundred implies that they were near six hundred, which, given the number of British in South Carolina at the time, would not be insignificant.
2. Rawdon to Cornwallis, May 24, 1781, in Saberton, *CP*, Vol. V, 288.
3. Rawdon to Balfour, May 15, 1781, *Papers of the Continental Congress* (Washington, DC) Item 155, Roll 175, Volume 2:95.
4. Colonel William R. Davie, "Recollection of a Conversation between General Nathanael Greene and Colonel William Davie, in, *GP*, Vol. VIII, 225; George W. Greene, *Life of Nathanael Greene* (Cranbury, NJ: The Scholar's Bookshelf, 2007, original 1864), 241–52.
5. Terry Golway, *Washington's General*, 270.
6. Howard to Johnson, undated [ca. 1822?], Lee Family Papers, Rocky Mount, VA. Both Henry Lee and William Johnson deny that Greene was depressed by events. Howard's letter to Johnson was in response to Johnson's statement "But we have conclusive evidence to show that General Greene never was dissatisfied with his movement to the south, and never contemplated a retreat before Camden in consequence of the affair of Hobkirk's Hill." See "Postscript," in William Johnson, *Sketches*, 8. Lee's son, Henry Jr., believed Davie "mistaken as to time and place," and that if Greene had expressed such "impressive and desponding language to Davie," it must have been April 25 after Hobkirk's Hill. See H. Lee, *The Campaign of 1781 in the Carolinas: with Remarks Historical and Critical of Johnson's Life of Greene* (Philadelphia, PA: E. Littell 1824), 360–61.
7. Whatever historians now think about Sumter, William Johnson in his early biography of Greene's life defended Sumter, noting, "No cause operated more strongly in forcing Rawdon to abandon the upper country and release the American commander from his accumulated embarrassments, than the progress made by Sumter in the middle country. Nor could Marion and Lee have securely carried on the contemporaneous and protracted siege of Fort Motte, had not the posts and the country above them been kept in check by the parties brought into the field by Sumpter." Johnson, *Sketches*, 106.
8. Ibid., 119.

Bibliography

Primary Sources

Accounts Audited (AA) of Claims Growing out of the Revolution in South Carolina, 1775–1856, South Carolina Department of Archives and History, Columbia.

Charleston Deed Books. South Carolina Department of Archives and History, Columbia, SC.

Clinton, Sir Henry. Clinton Papers. William Clements Library, University of Michigan, Ann Arbor.

Drayton, William. Remarks in a Tour Through the Back Country of the State of South Carolina, 1784. 34/0630, South Carolina Historical Society, Addlestone Library Archives, Charleston.

Draper, Lyman C. Thomas Sumter Papers in the Draper Manuscript Collection. Wisconsin Historical Society. Microfilm copies, South Carolina Department of Archives and History, Columbia.

Lamar, William. Nathanael Greene's Orderly Book, 5 April–4 September, MSS L200, Society of the Cincinnati, Washington, DC.

Lee Family Papers, Robert Alonzo Brock Collection, Huntington Library, San Marino, California.

Lee, Henry. Papers, Rocky Mount, VA.

List of Officers of the Army. London War Office, 1783.

MacClean, Hector. Orderly Book. Lieutenant Hector MacClean, 84th Infantry, William Clements Library, University of Michigan, Ann Arbor. Provided by Todd Braisted, July 23, 2013.

Marion, Francis. Orderly Book, 1775–1782. Huntington Library, San Marino, CA. (See also Published Primary Sources, O'Kelley.)

Mathis, Samuel. Samuel Mathis Papers, March–July 1781. South Caroliniana Library, University of South Carolina, Columbia.

Nase, Henry. Diary of Henry Nase, King's American Regiment, December 26, 1775, to January 29, 1784. Transcribed by Todd Braisted in 1991. Nase Family Papers, New Brunswick Museum, Archives Division, Saint John, New Brunswick.

Papers of the Continental Congress, National Archives, Washington, DC.

Pinckney, Thomas. Thomas Pinckney Papers. South Caroliniana Library, University of South Carolina, Columbia.

Pinckney Family Papers. Letter of Harriet Rutledge, October 9, 1855, attached to Letter of CC Pinkney, September 27, 1855. 43/1096. South Carolina Historical Society, Addlestone Library Archives, Charleston.

Probate Court Books. South Carolina Department of Archives and History, Columbia.

Revolutionary War Pension Applications. National Archives, Washington, DC.

South Carolina Probate Court Books. South Carolina Department of Archives and History, Columbia.

Saunders, John. 1754–1834. Saunders Papers, Loyalist Collection, Harriet C. Irving Library, University of New Brunswick, Fredericton, New Brunswick. Transcription courtesy Jim Piecuch.

Starcloff. Muster Roll for CPT Starcloff's Light Dragoons, Burgoyne Collection, Box 1, Folder 2. National Society of the Sons of the American Revolution, Louisville, KY.

Thomson, William. Papers, South Caroliniana Library, University of South Carolina, Columbia.

Published Primary Sources

Barnwell, Joseph W. "Letters to General Greene and Others." *South Carolina Historical Magazine*, XVII, no. 1 (1916): 3.

Clark, Walter, ed. *The State Records of North Carolina, Volume XVII, 1781–85.* Goldsboro, NC: Nash Bro. Book and Job Printers, 1899. Also, *Volume XIV, 1896.*

Conrad, Dennis M., Roger N. Parks, Martha J. King, and Richard K. Showman, eds. *The Papers of Nathanael Greene, Volume VIII, 30 March–10 July 1781.* Chapel Hill: The University of North Carolina Press, 1995.

Conrad, Dennis M., Roger N. Parks, and Martha J. King, eds. *The Papers of Nathanael Greene, Volume IX, 11 July 1781–2 December 1781.* Chapel Hill: The University of North Carolina Press, 1997.

Conrad, Dennis M., Roger N. Parks, and Elizabeth C. Stevens, eds. *The Papers of Nathanael Greene, Volume XII, 1 October 1782–21 May 1783.* Chapel Hill: The University of North Carolina Press, 2002.

Davies, K. G. *Documents of the American Revolution 1770–1783, Volume XX, Transcripts 1781.* Dublin, Ireland: Irish University Press, 1979.

Feltman, Lieut. William. *The Journal of Lieut. William Feltman, of the First Pennsylvania Regiment, 1781–1782.* Philadelphia: Henry Carey Baird for the Historical Society of Pennsylvania, 1853.

Gibbes, Robert W. *Documentary History of the American Revolution, Volume 1.* Columbia, SC: Banner Steam-Power Press, 1853.

O'Kelley, Patrick. *Unwaried Patience and Fortitude: Francis Marion's Orderly Book.* West Conshohocken, PA: Infinity Publishing Company, 2006.

Papers of the Revolutionary Era Pinckney Statemen. *The Papers of the Revolutionary Era Pinckney Statesmen Digital Edition,* ed. Constance B. Schulz. Charlottesville: University of Virginia Press, Rotunda, 2016, digital edition, https://rotunda.upress.virginia.edu/founders/PNKY-01-01-02-0007-0030.

Pinckney, Eliza Lucas. *The Papers of Eliza Lucas Pinckney and Harriott Pinckney Horry, Digital Edition,* ed. Constance B. Shulz, https://rotunda.upress.virginia.edu/PinckneyHorry/elp-details.xqy?letter=/PinckneyHorry/ELP0556.xml&return=toc_chron, accessed December 16, 2022.

Saberton, Ian, ed. *The Cornwallis Papers, The Campaigns of 1780 and 1781 in the Southern Theatre of the American Revolution, Volumes I through VI.* Uckfield, East Sussex, England: The Naval & Military Press, 2010.

Showman, Richard K., Dennis M. Conrad, and Roger N. Parks, Elizabeth C. Stevens, eds. *The Papers of General Nathanael Greene, Volume VI, 1 June 1780–25 December 1780.* Chapel Hill: The University of North Carolina Press, 1991.

Showman, Richard K., Dennis M. Conrad, Roger N. Parks, Elizabeth C. Stevens, eds. *The Papers of General Nathanael Greene, Volume VII, 25 December 1780–29 March 1781.* Chapel Hill: The University of North Carolina Press, 1994.

Secondary Sources

Babits, Lawrence. *A Devil of a Whipping: The Battle of Cowpens.* Chapel Hill: The University of North Carolina Press, 1998.

_______. "Hobkirk's Hill," in *Encyclopedia of the American Revolution.* New York: Thomson Gale Corporation, Volume 1, Second Edition, 2006.

_______. *"Perhaps the Most Important Victory of the Whole War,"* book manuscript in press.

Bass, Robert. *Swamp Fox: The Life and Campaigns of General Francis Marion.* New York: Henry Holt and Company, 1959.

_______. *Gamecock: The Life and Campaigns of General Thomas Sumter.* Orangeburg, SC: Sandlapper Publishing Co, 2000, original 1961.

Baxley, Bennett, ed. *St. James- Santee Parish Historical Sketches: Plantations, Churches, Villages, and Homes.* McClellanville, SC: St. James-Santee Parish Historical Society, 1997.

Boatner, Mark M. *Encyclopedia of the American Revolution.* Mechanicsburg, PA: Stackpole Books, 1994, original 1966.

Bridges, Anne B. L. and Roy Williams, III. *St James Santee Plantation Parish: History and Records, 1685–1925.* Spartanburg, SC: The Reprint Company, 1996.

Brooks, N. C. "Battle of Eutaw Springs." *Graham's Magazine,* Volume XVII, December 1845.

Buchanan, John. *The Road to Guilford Courthouse: The American Revolution in the Carolinas.* New York: John Wiley & Sons, 1997.

_______. *The Road to Charleston: Nathanael Greene and the American Revolution.* Charlottesville: University of Virginia Press, 2019.

Bull, Kinloch, Jr. *The Oligarchs in Colonial and Revolutionary Charleston: Lieutenant Governor William Bull II and His Family.* Columbia: University of South Carolina Press, 1991.

Cheves, Langdon. "Izards of South Carolina." *South Carolina Historical and Genealogical Magazine* Vol. 2, no. 3 (1901): 205–40.

Cote, Richard N. *Mary's World: Love, War, and Family Ties in Nineteenth Century Charleston.* Mount Pleasant, SC: Corinthian Books, 2001.

Daughters of the American Revolution. "Tablet to Mrs. Rebecca Motte." Program, D.A.R. Ceremony of Unveiling at St. Philips Church, Charleston, South Carolina, May 9th, 1903. Daggett Printing Company, 1903, on file, South Caroliniana Library.

Dornfest, Walter T. "John Watson Tadwell Watson and the Provincial Light Infantry, 1780–1781." *Journal of the Society for Army Historical Research* 75 (1997): 220–29. Revised, 2007 in *Southern Campaigns of the American Revolution,* April–June, no. 4, 2:47–64.

______. Military Loyalists of the American Revolution, 1775–1783. Jefferson, NC: McFarland & Company, Inc., 2011.

Dougherty, Kevin and Steven D. Smith. *Leading Like the Swamp Fox: The Leadership Lessons of Francis Marion.* Philadelphia, PA: Casemate Books, 2022.

Edgar, Walter B. and N. Louise Bailey. *Biographical Directory of the South Carolina House of Representatives, Volume II: The Commons House of Assembly 1692–1775.* Columbia: University of South Carolina Press, 1977.

Ferguson, Leland G. *Archeology at Scott's Lake, Exploratory Research 1972, 1973.* Columbia: Research Manuscript Series 68, South Carolina Institute of Archaeology and Anthropology, 1975.

_______. "An Archeological-Historical Analysis of Fort Watson: December 1780–April 1781." In *Research Strategies in Historical Archeology,* edited by Stanley South, 41–71. New York: Academic Press, 1977.

Fitzpatrick, John C., ed. *The Writings of George Washington, Volume 22, April 27, 1781–August 15, 1781.* Washington, DC: United States Printing Office, 1931.

Garden, Alexander. *Anecdotes of the Revolutionary War in America: With Sketches of Character of Persons the Most Distinguished, In the Southern States, For Civil and Military Service.* Charleston, SC: A. E. Miller, 1822.

Golway, Terry. *Washington's General: Nathanael Greene and the Triumph of the American Revolution.* New York: Henry Holt and Company, 2005.

Gordon, William. *The History of the Rise, Progress, and Establishment of the Independence of the United States of America,* Four Volumes. London, 1788.

Gregg, Alexander. *History of the Old Cheraws.* New York: Richardson and Company, 1867.

Grégorie, Anne King. *Thomas Sumter.* Columbia, SC: The R. L. Bryan Company, 1931.

Greene, George W. *Life of Nathanael Greene.* Cranbury, NJ: The Scholar's Bookshelf, 2007, original 1864.

Hambright, Ellan. Senior thesis, University of South Carolina, 2016.

Harris, C. Leon and Charles B. Baxley. "To Keep Up the Spirits of the People and Alarm the Enemy: Sumter's Rounds in South Carolina, February 16–March 9, 1781." *Southern Campaigns of the American Revolution* 20, no. 3 (2022).

Harrison, Margaret Hayne. *A Charleston Album.* Ringe, NH: Richard R. Smith Publications, Inc., 1953.

Helsley, Alexia Jones. *South Carolinians in the War for American Independence.* Columbia: South Carolina Department of Archives and History, 2000.

Horry, Peter and Parson M. L. Weems. *The Life of General Francis Marion: A Celebrated Partisan Officer, in the Revolutionary War, against the British and Tories in South Carolina and Georgia.* Philadelphia, PA: J. B. Lippincott, 1891. First edition, 1809.

James, William Dobein. *A Sketch of the Life of Brigadier General Francis Marion.* Charleston, SC: Gould and Riley, 1821. Reprint Marietta, GA: Continental Book Company, 1948.

Johnson, Joseph. *Traditions and Reminiscences Chiefly of the American Revolution.* Spartanburg, SC: The Reprint Company, 1972, original 1851.

Johnson, William. *Sketches of the Life and Correspondence of Nathanael Greene, Volumes I and II.* Charleston, SC: A.E. Miller, 1822.

Katcher, Philip R. N. *Encyclopedia of British, Provincial, and German Army Units, 1775–1783.* Harrisburg, PA: Stackpole Books, 1973.

Kolb, Wade S. III and Robert M. Weir. *Captured at Kings Mountain: The Journal of Uzal Johnson.* Columbia: University of South Carolina Press, 2011.

Lambert, Robert Stansbury. *South Carolina Loyalists in the American Revolution.* Columbia: University of South Carolina Press, 1987.

Lee, Henry, Jr. *The Campaign of 1781 in the Carolinas: with Remarks Historical and Critical of Johnson's Life of Greene.* Philadelphia, PA: E, Littell, 1824.

Lee, Robert E., ed. *The Revolutionary War Memoirs of General Henry Lee.* New York: DeCapo Press, 1998, original 1812 as *Memoirs of the War in the Southern Department of the United States.*

Leslie, Sir Stephen, ed. "Balfour, Nisbet." In *Dictionary of National Biography,* Volume III. London: Elder Smith & Company, 1885.

_______. "Hastings, Francis Rawdon." In *Dictionary of National Biography,* Volume XXV. London: Elder Smith & Company, 1891.

Lipscomb, Terry. *Revolutionary Battles, Skirmishes, and Actions in South Carolina.* Columbia: The South Carolina American Revolution Bicentennial Commission, n.d., ca. 1991.

_______. *Names In South Carolina,* Volume XXIV, on file, South Caroliniana Library, University of South Carolina.

Lockhart, Mathew A. "Sumter, Thomas." In *The South Carolina Encyclopedia,* edited by Walter Edgar, 940–41. Columbia: The University of South Carolina Press, 2006.

Lossing, Benson J. *Pictorial Field-Book of the Revolution,* original 1850, 2004 edition edited by Jack E. Fryar Jr. Wilmington, NC: Dram Tree Books, Inc., 2004.

_______. *Reflections of Rebellion Hours With the Living Men and Women of the Revolution.* Charleston, SC: The History Press, 2005, original 1889.

Mabelitini, Charles Brian. "British Fortification Strategy in the South Carolina Backcountry During the Southern Campaign of the American Revolution: Archaeological and Historical Perspectives on Infrastructure and Landscape." PhD diss., University of South Carolina, 2024.

MacKenzie, Roderick. *Strictures on Lt. Col. Tarleton's History of the Campaigns of 1780 and 1781, in the Southern Provinces of North America.* London: R. Faulder, 1787.

Massey, Gregory D. "Pinckney, Thomas." In *South Carolina Encyclopedia,* edited by Walter Edgar, 731–32. Columbia: University of South Carolina Press, 2006).

McCrady, Edward. *The History of South Carolina in the Revolution, 1780–1783.* New York: MacMillan, 1902.

Mills, Robert. *Mills' Atlas of the State of South Carolina.* Greenville, SC, Reprint 1980, Southern Historical Press, original 1825.

Moss, Bobby Gilmore. *Roster of South Carolina Patriots in the American Revolution.* Baltimore, MD: Genealogical Publishing Co., 1983.

Names in South Carolina, Volume XII. South Caroliniana Library, University of South Carolina, Columbia.

Nelson, Paul David. "Rawdon-Hastings, Francis." In *Encyclopedia of the American Revolution, Second Edition, Volume 2,* editor in chief Harold E. Selesky, 966–68. New York: Thomson Gale, 2006.

O'Kelley, Patrick. *Unwaried Patience and Fortitude: Francis Marion's Orderly Book.* Conshohocken, PA: Infinity Publishing, 2006.

Oliphant, John. "Cornwallis, Charles." In *Encyclopedia of the American Revolution, Second Edition, Volume 1,* editor in chief Harold E. Selesky, 271–75. New York: Thomson Gale, 2006.

Oller, John. *The Swamp Fox: How Francis Marion Saved the American Revolution.* New York: Da Capo Press, 2016.

Palmer, Gregory. *Biographical Sketches of Loyalists of the American Revolution.* Westport, CT: Meckler Publishing, 1984.

Pickett, Margaret F. *Rebecca Brewton Motte: American Patriot and Successful Rice Planter.* Charleston, SC: Evening Post Books, 2022.

Pinckney, Charles Cotesworth. *Life of General Thomas Pinckney.* Boston, MA: Houghton, Mifflin and Company, 1895.

Pinckney, Elise. "Letters of Eliza Lucas Pinckney, 1768–1782." *South Carolina Historical Magazine* 76, no. 3 (1975): 143–70.

Ramsay, David. *History of the Revolution of South Carolina From a British Province To An Independent State.* Trenton, [NJ?]: Isaac Collins, 1785.

Rankin, Hugh. "Charles Lord Cornwallis: Study in Frustration." In *George Washington's Opponents: British Generals in the American Revolution,* edited by George Athan Billias, 193–232. New York: William Morrow and Company, Inc., 1969.

_______. *Francis Marion: The Swamp Fox.* New York: Thomas Y. Crowell, 1973.

_______. *The North Carolina Continentals.* Chapel Hill: The University of North Carolina Press, 1971.

Royster, Charles. "Introduction." In *The Revolutionary War Memoirs of General Henry Lee*, edited by Robert E. Lee, iii–ix. New York: De Capo Press, 1998.

Rudisill, Horace Fraser. *The Diaries of Evan Pugh (1762–1801)*. Florence, SC: St. David's Society, 1993.

Saberton, Ian. "Biographical Sketches of Royal Militia Commanders In The South Carolina Mid-and Lowcountry, North Carolina, and Georgia, 1780–82." *Journal of the American Revolution*. Accessed, May 12, 2022. https://allthingsliberty.com/2020/12/biographical-sketches-of-royal-militia-commanders-in-the-south-carolina-mid-and-lowcountry-north-carolina-and-georgia-1780-82/.

Salley, Alexander. *The History of Orangeburg County, South Carolina*. Orangeburg, SC: R. Lewis Berry Printer, 1898.

______. "Col. Miles Brewton and Some of His Descendants." *South Carolina Historical and Genealogical Magazine* 2, no. 2 (1901): 130–31, 142–44, 148–50.

Shepherd, Rebecca E. "Going Up Country: A Comparison of Elite Ceramic Consumption Patterns in Charleston and the Carolina Frontier." Master's thesis, University of South Carolina, 2014.

Simms, William Gilmore. *The Life of Francis Marion*. New York: G. F. Cooledge & Brother, 1844.

Smith, Henry A. M. "The Upper Ashley; and the Mutations of Families." *South Carolina Historical and Genealogical Magazine* 20, no. 3 (1919): 151–98.

Smith, Steven D. *Francis Marion and the Snow's Island Community: Myth, History, and Archaeology*. Asheville, NC: United Writers Press, Inc., 2021.

______. "A Spoof on Francis Marion, the Swamp Fox." *Military Collector & Historian*, 67, no. 4 (2015): 357–58.

Smith, Steven D., James B. Legg, Tamara S. Wilson, and Jonathan Leader. "'Obstinate and Strong': The History and Archaeology of the Siege of Fort Motte." Columbia: South Carolina Institute of Archaeology and Anthropology, 2007.

Smith, Steven D., Brian Mabelitini, James B. Legg, and Ellan Hambright. "Two Revolutionary War Expedient Fire Arrows From Archaeological Contexts in South Carolina. *Journal of the Company of Military Historians* 71, no. 3 (2019): 243–46.

Tarleton, Lieutenant Colonel Banastre. *A History of the Campaigns of 1780 and 1781 in the Southern Provinces of North America.* Cranbury NJ: The Scholar's Bookshelf, 2005, original 1787.

Weslin, Mrs. O. J. and Miss Anges Irvin. *Worthy Women of Our First Century.* Philadelphia, PA: J. B. Lippenwith Co., 1877.

Williams, Francis Leigh. *A Founding Family: The Pinckneys of South Carolina.* New York: Harcourt Brace Jovanovich, 1978.

Whitacre, Stacey R. "An Analysis of Lead Shot From Fort Motte, 2004–2012: Assessing Combat Behavior in Terms of Agency." Master's thesis, University of South Carolina, 2013.

Wright, Robert K., Jr. *The Continental Army.* Washington, DC: Center of Military History, United States Army, 1983.

Other Sources

84th Reg't, Royal Highland Emigrants, https://www.84th-rhe.com/. Accessed, July 13, 2023.

"Garrison Orders." *Royal Gazette,* May 30, 1781.

Rawdon, Francis. Post, May 14, 1781. *Royal Gazette,* June 6th, 1781.

Lewis, J. D. "The Evolution of Marion's Brigade After the Fall of Charleston 1780 to 1782." Slide presentation, www.carolana.com.

Letter, Chas. McPherson to Major Maxwell, May 5, 1781. Auction Lot 6, Fall Historical Auction Sale, Alexander Historical Auctions, Stamford, CT, October 9, 2010, copy in author's possession.

Smith, Levi. "To the Printers of the Royal Gazette." *Royal Gazette,* Charleston, SC, April 17, 1782.

Royal Gazette, March 13, 1782.

Southern Literary Gazette, "The Swamp Fox." 1829.

Acknowledgments

All authors rely on many individuals who make their books better, more readable, more accurate, and more attractive. That the archaeological remains of Fort Motte still exist is due to the Wannamaker family, especially Luther and Doraine Wannamaker, who first allowed me to work at the site in 2004 and have been great friends and supporters ever since. I thank Mark Lender and Martin James for reviewing the book and offering excellent suggestions, and to Bruce H. Franklin for publishing the result. An excellent final copyedit was provided by Ms. Christine Florie. Historians, archaeologists, and researchers who assisted me include Lawrence Babits, Tom Braisted, Charles Baxley, Tommy Charles, Chris Clement, Josh Howard, Nicholas Hobar, David Neilan, John Oller, Margaret Pickett, Jim Piecuch, David Reuwer, Kim Stacey, Chris Swager, Sean Taylor, Richard Watkins, Rick Wise, and Martha Zierden. Special thanks to Sam Fore for all the friendship, insights, and discoveries through the years. Among many detectorists who worked at the site, Spencer Barker, Stacey Whitacre, and Brett Collin stand out. A good edit of the draft was provided by Heathley Johnson, funded by the South Carolina Archaeological Research Trust. Archaeologist John Fisher drafted the maps for the book. Long-time colleague and co-conspirator James B. Legg conducted most of the archaeological work at the site of Fort Motte with me since 2004 and contributed many thoughts herein. A sincere thanks to Albert Zambone, who was offered the chance to write on Fort Motte and was kind enough to ask me first if I was working on a book and then allowed me to intercede. None of these individuals are responsible for any errors in the book—those I reserve for myself with humble apology, *ad maiorem Dei gloriam.*

Index